GOWLAND'S GUIDE To GLAMOUR PHOTOGRAPHY

GOWLAND'S GUIDE To GLAMOUR PHOTOGRAPHY

BY PETER GOWLAND

CROWN PUBLISHERS, INC., NEW YORK

Also by the author

HOW TO PHOTOGRAPH WOMEN
STEREO PHOTOGRAPHY
FIGURE PHOTOGRAPHY
HOW TO TAKE BETTER HOME MOVIES
GLAMOUR TECHNIQUES
FACE AND FIGURE
GLAMOUR CAMERA
PHOTO SECRETS
ELECTRONIC FLASH GUIDE
PHOTO IDEAS
THE FIGURE
CAMERA IN HAWAII
CAMERA IN THE ORIENT

Library of Congress Catalog Card Number: 76–185079
ISBN: 0-517-501899

Printed in the United States of America
Published simultaneously in Canada by General Publishing
Company Limited

20 19 18 17 16 15

Contents

1

How I Got Started in Glamour Photography

The question I am asked most often is how I got started in glamour photography, so I thought a chapter on the subject might save me a great deal of future correspondence. Also, it might help those who are interested in getting into this field. Included here is advice on the different markets and means of selling glamour.

I've been taking pictures since I was thirteen years old. I had several makeshift darkrooms (in bathrooms, bedrooms, backyards) before I built what I would call an efficient, almost professional one. I converted into a very spacious darkroom one bedroom of a two-bedroom house that I rented in Hollywood, where I worked in motion pictures as an extra. Since movie people always need pictures, I earned additional money by photographing fellow employees. I used the living room as a studio for shooting indoor portraits. Looking at some of the negatives today I am still amazed at their quality.

There were lots of pretty girls working as extras, and they were much more fun to photograph than men. Naturally I built up a rapport with women, which helped me more than anything else to become known as a photographer of women. I also took many pictures of children, animals, houses, and scenery, but my specialty remained women.

When I married Alice, she knew nothing about the techniques of photography, but she had an eye for pictures and a keen desire to learn. I taught her darkroom work and tried to teach her to take pictures. She was never very interested in the actual manipulation of the camera, preferring to direct. However, she does take pictures when the fancy strikes her, and I'm glad that she finally learned about f stops, shutter speeds, light meters, etc.

Alice also can type and write letters and do short background pieces to accompany pictures. She studied the various markets, and while I was in the Army for thirteen months she managed to sell a couple of 4 x 5 color shots we had taken together just before I sailed for Germany. These were my first color pin-ups and are no different from those I take today, except in hair style and costume. Even so, they aren't that different, and if you avoid dating, a picture of a pretty girl will always sell.

After the Army, we had saved enough money to buy a small commercial lot, on which we built a studio twenty-two feet wide and a hundred feet long, not caring to go into heavy debt just to create a prosperous front. We lived in the rear of the building. I continued working as an extra and took portrait sittings on my days off.

Markets have changed drastically since I was a beginner, so the person going into this field today will have a different challenge. While restrictions on nudity have been lifted to a great extent, there are hundreds of glamour photographers to compete with. But there are also more outlets for this type of work. Even the fashion magazines are more daring in their use of artistic nudes in their advertising and editorial pages.

The following points are of great importance in becoming a successful glamour photographer:

Choice of Model.   Not everyone knows a good model when he sees one. First, you have to be aware of the type of girl sought in the different markets. (See Chapter 4 on models.)

Technical Quality.   The successful glamour photographer must be able to create exciting, provocative pictures and still maintain technical quality.

The most lucrative assignments are made in the commercial advertising field. When a client wants a photograph of his product with a pretty girl, you can be sure the product has to be sharp, well lighted, and at its most flattering angle. Photographs taken in a studio are much easier to control, as far as lighting and exposure and other technicalities are concerned. But suppose your client wants a picture of a girl running in the surf, at late sunset, feet splashing (stop action), with flash, in color—and in black and white. That takes more than just knowing how to direct a model. (See Chapter 11 on action.)

This pin-up, taken over twenty years ago, is almost dateless. Bikinis in those days were rare, but today this would not be brief enough.

The choice of a model is very important. Here, Leigh Christian typifies the kind of natural beauty that is most important for glamour work. Make-up may help, but it never should be depended upon to make an unglamorous girl glamorous.

Andria Blahd is definitely a fashion model. Her thin figure does not lend itself to pin-ups, but in clothes, such as here, in youthful girdles and bras, and as a semi-nude for high-fashion ads, she is excellent.

In commercial advertising a client may want a photograph of his product with a pretty girl, so technical quality is essential.

Be Prolific.   Don't wait for assignments. Take pictures as often as you can find a good model. But when working on speculation, be aware of the markets that are available. In shooting for calendar companies, there are certain rules that almost never change. Outdoor pictures must have a blue sky and they prefer a selection of both horizontal and vertical views of the same subject. These are general, and each company has its own specific requirements. Magazine editors buy picture sequences more often than a single photo. They are more apt to purchase a series that has some story content.

Build a Stock File.   In building your stock file, as you hear or read of different market requirements, add that particular category to your shooting schedule. All speculative shooting should be carefully filed so that it is easy to find either by model's name or by subject.

I've had good luck with building a stock file of glamour photos. About fourteen years ago Alice and I decided that there had to be an easier way to

Take pictures that are different and do so as often as possible. This picture of Mary Francis was taken on a speculative basis, but to date it has been used in several ads.

Romantic couples are always good subjects. I'm constantly on the lookout for handsome couples and often take them on a speculative basis, as was done here. A picture from the same sitting was used in an eyelash advertisement.

When photographing a girl for your own file, take as many changes of costume and location as you can work into the day, thus building up a variety of pictures that can be sold either as a group or singly.

get our pictures around. We had been doing only the few assignments that came to us through our pictures in the photography magazines and glamour books. It was a nuisance to send out proofs of the various girls and to keep track of them. So we compiled the best group of pictures from each girl's file and pasted them up to make a catalog. We sent these catalogs to at least 3,000 advertising agencies, asking that they keep it on file as a reference when they needed stock photographs. From this we received many new clients, and we are on our seventh catalog.

There are several advantages to the stock photo catalog. One of the best is taking only whatever picture inspires us. Also, we can do our own layouts and work in complete freedom from art directors and clients breathing down our necks. Not that it really bothers me to have these people around; I kind of like it, but the models sometimes freeze and are not as easy to work with.

I think this catalog idea on a small scale is a good means of advertising for the beginner who has talent and the ability to fill assignments but has no way of making his work known. Rather than calling on the agencies in person, let the U.S. Mail be your leg-man. A small brochure, beautifully printed and nicely laid out, with a selection of your best work, should bring returns.

Publicity.   Always try for name credit. The more your name is seen by art directors and ad agencies, the better chance you have of getting good assignments. The photography magazines always give name credit to photographers and often run portfolios on new and interesting ones. *Popular Photography* has always been a good outlet for me. One of my first covers was on that magazine. It was a picture of my young daughter with her puppy. Many times I would take less money for a job just to get my name on the pictures.

While traveling in Australia, I photographed this tan young lady on one of the stark white beaches and put it into my file of stock photographs.

Examples of stock photo-
graphs that can be easily sold
for commercial advertising:
plain backgrounds or beach
scenes.

This type of model is excellent for calendar-figure studies or artistic nudes. The beauty of both face and figure is an asset.

Having a woman partner helped in the selection of models because men are apt to get carried away by a girl's charms and forget whether or not she is photogenic. Alice and I found that over the years we can safely go on our very first impression. Our office looks out over our driveway, and when a prospective model arrives, we watch her step out of her car. At that moment we can pretty well tell if we will be using her or not. So many of my "scouts" are amazed when I tell them I consider the face first. Too often I receive a telephone call from some eager person who thinks he has a real find, but all he quotes are measurements. He's at a loss when I ask about the face!

I've always enjoyed the technical as much as the artistic end of photography. It led to my designing and manufacturing the Gowlandflex 4 x 5 and 5 x 7 twin-lens camera. I found that many of my clients liked candid quality, but also that they preferred the larger film either for retouching or better reproduction. But the view cameras were cumbersome and slow.

I spent many evenings in my garage-workshop designing the first Gowlandflex. It was then made of wood and covered with leather. When other photographers saw it they asked me to make one for them. I made ten, then one hundred. Finally I redesigned it as a metal camera for easier manufacturing. (All this time I was photographing girls.) I liked the idea of the large negative with the candid quality, and I use this format for most of my commercial accounts. I've also kept up a keen interest in lighting and have gone from floods, to flash, to strobe, and lately, to bounce using the Larson Reflectasols (see Chapters 6, 7). Just being interested in photographing girls isn't enough. The photographer has to take a keen interest in the technical end. He must know his equipment and keep up with new trends.

Many beginners in the field take a series of pictures of a girl and wait for them to sell. This is the easiest way to become discouraged. Send them out, then get busy with other pictures. Even today, I feel that I do not devote enough time to picture taking. I spend too much time in the office and the shop, whereas when I first went into business I was shooting nearly every day, sometimes on Saturdays. New pictures, new models, and new faces are always needed. And when taking new pictures, try new and varied techniques as well; I have even branched out into motion pictures in the last five years. Many cinematographers began as still photographers, and the cinema now uses the techniques of the still man. The broader your vision, the more creative you will become with your photography.

Many of my assignments are difficult because they require physical labor. This picture was taken on a 90-degree day when the models had to work in hot clothing. Artificial snow was carted to the scene in a huge box and dumped onto a sheet so that I could take it back with me. Note the use of the reflector to offset the harsh shadows cast by the high sun.

In 1957 I began manufacturing the Gowland-flex camera because I liked to take many of my commercial assignments on the larger film format. Since then I have produced and sold about 300 Gowlandflex cameras. The reflector is the 36-inch Larson Reflectasol.

A community project to save the beach utilized my talent as a cinematographer and Alice's as a writer-producer. We're photographing Sue Beck and James Ashley as they run along the shoreline.

2

On Cameras and Developing

Most photographers who are interested in glamour already know the basic elements of photography, such as the explanation of f stops and shutter speeds, ASA numbers, and the functions of the various lenses. For those who do not, I will review most of these fundamentals but the thrust of the book will be to specifics relative to glamour.

It would be impossible to explore all the cameras on the market today and all the various developing techniques, films, papers, and lighting. I will cover those that I use and find to be the most appropriate for photographing women. There may be other equipment, developers, and techniques that are preferred, but that is a matter of individual taste. I can only hope to guide the interested person by dealing with the specific equipment and experiences that created the pictures in this book.

HASSELBLAD 500 C

I consider the 2¼ x 2¼ format a compromise between 35mm and 4 x 5. It gives fine grain, large proofs, and a negative that can be printed over and over with a minimum of scratches.

For my 2¼ work I use the Hasselblad 500 C because I like the interchangeable lenses and backs (magazines). With two magazines and two different focal-length lenses it is like having four cameras in one. Each lens gives a different perspective to my pictures—from portrait close-ups,

In the past few years I have expanded into motion pictures, working as a cameraman on Wide World of Sports and on several independent sports productions. I like it because it's a challenge and a change. In the horse scene I'm using a 400-foot magazine with the 16mm movie camera.

with background thrown out of focus, to full lengths. By having two backs, an assistant can load one while I am shooting, thus saving valuable time. An alternative, equally valuable, is to load one magazine with color and the other with black and white.

Another feature that made me choose the Hasselblad over other 2¼ x 2¼ cameras was the Compur, a between-the-lens shutter. A between-the-lens shutter is located in the lens and exposes the entire piece of film during the exposure from 1 second to 1/500 second. Most cameras in the 2¼ x 2¼ single-lens class have focal plane shutters. A focal-plane shutter is a curtain with variable size slits that is located next to the film. As the slit passes next to the film it exposes only a portion at a time. The between-the-lens shutter can synchronize with flash at all speeds while the focal-plane shutter can synchronize at only one speed (usually 1/60 second). Since I do so much action work with models at the beach and other outdoor locations, it is important to use the between-the-lens shutter that can synchronize with all speeds.

Because I don't want to be bogged down with unnecessary equipment (too many cameras and too many lenses only lead to confusion), I have cut down to one Hasselblad body, two backs, and two lenses for my 2¼ work. I have the normal 80mm f/2.8 Zeiss Planar and the 150mm f/4 Zeiss Sonnar. The normal 80mm lens is used on full lengths and the 150mm is used for portraits. I have decided on the 150mm over the 250mm lens because it is one stop faster, allowing me to work with half the light or to hand-hold the

The Hasselblad sits on the floor while I set up an umbrella reflector.

◄

I used the Hasselblad with 150mm lens for this portrait of a lovely French actress, Marie Boyer. It was taken in a hotel room in Paris, using window light only.

camera where I would otherwise have to use a tripod. It can also be used in close quarters, whereas the 250mm requires a greater distance from the model.

An advantage to using the telephoto lens with the 2¼ negative is that it is possible to make a portrait image on the film large enough to retouch. I try to fill the negative area with the face so that the retoucher has about a two-inch head to work with. This can be done when using the 150mm or 250mm lens. Sometimes I use extension tubes to get larger heads and carry the 21mm and 55mm tubes in my Vivitar aluminum carrying case. There is room also for the 70mm Hasselblad back; it gives me 80 exposures on a single roll. I load my own film from 100-foot rolls of Kodak Plus-X, which saves me money and I get more exposures per roll.

In this same case I carry the extra Hasselblad back, the Pentax spot meter, Wein flash meter, regular 80mm lens shade, and a professional lens shade. (I use the latter for back-lighted pictures when strong backlight on the model may be shining into the camera lens.)

PENTAX CAMERAS

I prefer to use 35mm film when I want a more candid feeling, or when working in less light, or when I want the advantages of using Kodachrome II over Ektachrome. Kodachrome II is much better for making prints.

My Pentax equipment is varied because I use it on other assignments as well as glamour. But here, too, one could get by with less. A basic beginning would be a 55mm and a 105mm lens and one camera body; one can build on these later with wider angle or longer focal lengths.

Gowland and Gowlandflex.

Here I'm setting up a scene with my Pentax suspended from my neck.

Pentax is the world's most popular single-lens 35mm camera. It has lenses as sharp as the more expensive cameras, can take more lenses because it uses the simple screw mount, and is smaller and lighter than the more expensive single-lens reflexes. The meter is built in, avoiding having a huge projection on the top. In short, Pentax is the best camera in the 35mm field for the money.

THE GOWLANDFLEX

In 1956 I built my first Gowlandflex, a twin-lens 4 x 5 format camera, because of the many clients who requested (and still do) large color and shunned 35mm and 2¼ transparencies. To shoot 4 x 5 with a view camera is

▶

The Pentax camera with 35mm lens was used here. Australia is not known for its waterfalls, so the model was posed below to show the full beauty of the nude as well as the environment.

like going back a hundred years! The Gowlandflex allows me to use large film for hand-held pictures of models even in the splashing surf with the same ease as my smaller cameras. I have always preferred to view the composition, expression, and focus on the ground glass right-side up as I have done with the Pentax, Hasselblad, and Rollei, the last influencing my design of the Gowlandflex. Now I can do the same with the Gowlandflex. Many photographers use the Gowlandflex with 2¼ x 2¾ roll film backs so they can use the longer lenses and make 16 x 20 color prints of portraits.

ON DEVELOPING AND PRINTING

Whether or not you do your own developing and printing should depend on how serious you are about your photography and what you intend to do with it. Speaking now of black and white only, I believe that it is of great help to a beginner to develop and print his own negatives. In this way he can understand his mistakes and learn firsthand what the various techniques produce. At one time I did all my own black and white developing and printing. Now I have a capable and creative assistant who does the darkroom work. We have strict rules about the handling and filing of negatives and have standards to meet in printing also. To me, taking the picture is only the beginning. Taking care of the negatives so that they do not get scratched or dusty is of equal importance to the finished picture.

But suppose you cannot afford a darkroom. There are many commercial labs both for color and black and white that do excellent work in developing and printing. As long as you maintain a good filing system for your negatives, it is possible to get fine results from these labs. Recently, some labs have come out with everything the amateur needs for his own darkroom work. For a small fee you can rent these darkrooms for several hours, or by the day. There is usually professional advice available.

The most rewarding way, however, is to do your own work, especially if you have the time. Here you have complete control. If a print is too gray, you can use a more contrasting paper. If cropping helps, you can use your own feeling about where it should be changed. I have known many photographers who ended up being specialists in the printing and developing end. In my business I do not have the time to devote to the darkroom and only do printing on special occasions. In the meantime, I leave that to a specialist.

In the color area the labs with automated control are everywhere. Prices are so reasonable that it is hardly worthwhile to buy the chemicals and paper and equipment necessary for this process. Color people, too, have become specialists in their field.

I do not need color prints in my business because most of my clients work from the transparencies. I do have display prints made for my office and for shows, and these are usually 16 x 20 or 11 x 14. The balance of my color work, the developing of the transparencies, is done by Roger Davidson, a photographer in his own right who now prefers to do lab work. He is a genius when it comes to this, and he has a completely automated lab not too far from my place. I shoot in the daytime and take the film to him at night where it is developed and ready for pick-up the next morning. Much better than when I had to mix chemicals and do the processing myself!

Practically all my black and white film is developed in the old standby D-76 solution, which my assistant and I mix ourselves. Developing time is usually only 8 minutes for 120 Verichrome Pan and Tri-X. We develop 70mm Plus-X in Polydol, also for 8 minutes.

We use Nikor reels for all the 35mm, 2¼, and 70mm film. The 22-inch Nikor tanks can develop 8 rolls of 120 film or 14 rolls of 35mm at one time with one gallon of developer. By using one tank for developer, one for stop bath, one for hypo, and the other for the storage of a second batch of undeveloped film, we can run through 16 rolls of 120 film in a very few minutes.

Our most popular printing paper is Du Pont Velour Black, single-weight glossy or double-weight glossy (dried matte). We stock grades 2, 3, and 4. On special high-contrast glamour assignments we use Agfa Brovira Glossy no. 6. Negatives shot on Kodak 2475 Recording Film with ASA 1000 are printed on this paper, giving excessive grain. The film is developed in DK-50.

When I find a paper and developer I like, I stick with it for a long time. I do the same with film and cameras. In this way I am free to create when taking the pictures. I do change, but only after much use, and this is the advice I would give to others. Don't jump around from one thing to another until you have first exhausted all possibilities.

3

Do You Need
a Studio?

One leading U.S. photographer in the field of glamour and journalism has never had a photographic studio. Though a studio definitely makes things easier, it is not obligatory for glamour photography.

Almost as good as a studio is a room at home. Indoor portraits can be made in any part of the house, with any type of lighting, because they encompass little of the body and require no extensive backgrounds. You can make beautiful portraits with just window light and a kicker fill-in—reflector, flood or spotlight (see Chapters 6, 7). For a dramatic effect, use no fill-in at all.

Window seats are a favorite method of utilizing window light. They are easy to improvise, too. I've built several in a matter of minutes. Of course the better ones take a little time. I keep on hand a quilted pad and material to match. The pad is the width of my bedroom window, and I formed a seat from two pieces of plywood and some braces which can be put into place quickly. The extra piece of material is pulled tightly over the base and the pad is placed on top. One could never tell that it is not a regular built-in seat.

Such a set-up affords many poses for a model to assume, and it gets away from the standing positions.

In using the home for glamour pictures it is very important that it be well designed, preferably light in color; small windows and dark wood paneling are unsatisfactory. My house was built to my photographic needs. It is

A white paper roll pulled down over a room area makes an instant studio for nude studies of Candace Thayer. Lighting was achieved with a large reflector bouncing a strobe from the right and a separate bounce strobe on the background.

basically white with a great deal of window area and plants and furniture that lend themselves to posed pictures. But because I have photographed it extensively, I try to borrow the houses of friends, those I find particularly beautiful. Even though the model is the main element in the pictures, she is enhanced by beautiful surroundings.

One friend in particular, an interior decorator, has a beautiful apartment filled with antique treasures and furnished with plush chairs, sofas,

By throwing the background out of focus with the 85mm lens on the Pentax, the model stands out from the foliage. The edge-lighting on her face and body add to this distinction. A reflector fill-in was used.

Erline Erskine lies down on a windowsill for this head-and-shoulders shot, and by over-exposing the background, a lovely profile study is obtained. Hasselblad with 250mm lens.

With just window light and a kicker fill-in.

◀
Working in Australia I used the bedroom of this lovely model as a background for the semi-nude study. Pentax with 55mm lens and window light only.

Model Patti Connelly poses in window-seat area of a home. Overexposed background permits her figure to stand out against both the curtains (opposite) and the windowpanes and foliage (above). Hasselblad with 80mm lens. One floodlight was used in the kneeling scene. Note the window has been blocked out with a screen. A reading with an exposure meter was taken of the background light area and the camera was then set at an f stop between these two extremes.

The bedroom curtains make an excellent background for this semi-nude study of Candace Thayer. Hasselblad with 80mm lens and daylight only.

A paper roll pulled down over a living room area and a chest of clothing as a prop make an excellent background for a nude study. A black paper background with a 1000-watt quartz light hitting it created a white area behind the model's black hat, making it stand out from the background. Window light from the right and floodlight from the left illuminate the model.

By overexposing the background, this room setting makes a nice area for a portrait of Betty Samuelson with an antique clock. Hasselblad with 80mm lens and daylight only.

This photo of Jeanne Rainier could have been shot anywhere. It was taken in a bedroom near a plain wall with a 75-watt bulb at a distance so as to simulate candlelight. Hasselblad with 250mm lens.

and so on. In addition to using his apartment, I have taken pieces of his furniture home so as to isolate a particular piece with my model. If such friends with houses and furnishings are not available, and your own place is decorated rather modestly, concentrate on areas where this will not make much difference. For example, the bedroom. By placing the model on the bed and shooting down—where the background becomes only the area of the bed—one needs only a good-looking bedspread. If you want to shoot with the camera at waist level, then you must make sure that the back-

This portrait, taken on white shag rug with a single light from one side, shows Shelly Green. The high angle and close-up create a dramatic effect. Hasselblad with 80mm lens.

ground does not interfere. Either a plain wall, or the headboard and wall would be a safe angle.

Don't limit your poses. Try different, even oddball, situations: the model on her stomach, with head falling over the foot of the bed, and hands extended to the floor, or the reverse—on her back with her head hanging over the edge. These make good close-ups and semi close-ups, as well as full-length pictures.

Another part of the bedroom that lends itself to pictures is the carpeted floor. Here, again, a high angle is best, leaving the rug area as a plain background.

Bathrooms, when roomy enough and pretty enough, give an opportunity to do nude pictures or semi-nude studies. If you can find a sunken tub, or an old-fashioned tub with legs, which is even better, you can't miss. Head and shoulder portraits in a foamy tub!

The difficulty encountered could be lighting. Generally, bathrooms have little, if any, available light. Sometimes the space can be so cramped as to make it almost impossible to bring additional lighting into play. Here is where I resort to bounce light, either flash or flood. Most bathrooms have

Using a bounce 1000-watt light in small area, such as the bathroom.

light-colored ceilings and it is possible to bounce the light through the door-way onto the ceiling. This gives a nice, soft, over-all illumination.

Kitchens, as a rule, are good only for a picture series where you want to show a variety of activities. Cooking might be one. They get a little on the posey side. But there may be areas in a kitchen that would be good for close-ups or semi close-ups.

It is possible to create a makeshift studio if you have a room that can be cleared of furniture easily. Paper rolls and Polecats make up the background. Polecats are aluminum poles that are easily secured between ceiling and floor. A spring in one end and a rubber tip at the other to prevent marring the ceiling and to aid in stability make it possible to adjust the poles to whatever height the room may be. Once these poles are put into place, an additional aluminum pole serves to hold the paper rolls that are mounted between the upright poles.

It will be necessary to use some form of artificial light, either flood, flash, or strobe. Here, again, the Polecats come in handy, as you can clip lights to them with brackets.

While building my present studio I made this set-up in the small living room of a cottage we had rented temporarily (although Polecats were not available at that time), and I'm sure that from the pictures taken no one would even guess they weren't from a commercial studio.

The basic difference is the convenience of having lights and backgrounds set up at all times rather than having to move furniture.

Another method of achieving a studio look is by placing the Polecats outdoors and hanging paper backgrounds to take advantage of sunlight. There are portable Polecats made especially for this. I've done this on several occasions and like the results, but it has the disadvantage of contending with such problems as wind (which can disturb the paper backgrounds).

Three paper rolls on Polecats—2 x 3s held secure with Timber Toppers at the ceiling. Lights can be suspended from a boom attached to one of the 2 x 3s. Toppers have spring-loaded metal boxes at the tops and are covered with rubber and fit over the poles. One-inch dowels inserted in bored holes in the poles hold the paper rolls.

Merci Montello poses against a white paper-roll background, but this could have been taken against a plain wall area of any home. A single bounce strobe light was used.

This is how you can use Polecats
outdoors—before and after.

These two pictures were taken in a patio. A white plastic screen was placed behind to hide distracting objects and the foliage. Hasselblad camera with 250mm lens and daylight only.

No studio was necessary for this picture taken in the shallow surf with Hasselblad held overhead. Sunlight only. Judy Meadows is the lovely model. Note high angle and consequent control of background.

Working outdoors in and along a stream, the model in both scenes is in shade. Reflected light is from a Reflectasol bouncing sunlight. Pentax with 55mm lens.

4

What Is a
Good Model?

A glamour picture is no better than the model. If you are
not used to taking glamour pictures, finding and judging whether or not a
girl would make a good model is not always easy. This might be the biggest
drawback if you are just starting with glamour subjects.

It can be very discouraging to try to photograph a girl who lacks confi-
dence in her own appearance and ability to pose. Also, if the picture is to be
sold, you have to be aware of what is appealing to the general public rather
than your own personal taste. When discussing what makes a good model, it
will be on the basis of what type of girl would be commercially saleable
rather than a personal preference.

Over the years I have found that girls who study dancing or who are
basically active are easier to photograph. They have good figures as a rule
and a natural ability to fall into graceful positions. Even so, these girls must
also be pretty. A good figure without a pretty face is not going to make a
successful picture.

Models seem to fall into various categories, which is one reason why it
is not possible to generalize about who will make a good model. It depends
on what type of picture is desired. There are basically four categories:

Face Models.   Here we have the girl who has outstanding features
—well-proportioned facial structure with large clear eyes, nicely shaped
nose, even white teeth, and a beautiful complexion. Before wigs and falls

Cheryl Anderson has perfect features for any type of portrait work. Large blue eyes, small, well-shaped nose, white even teeth, a beautiful complexion, and healthy hair. She is also tall and slender and so she is used for full-length fashion work as well. Hasselblad with 250mm lens.

Dancers make excellent subjects either for studio action or outdoor locations, as Brooke Mills demonstrates with a dance on the wet sand at Santa Monica beach. Pentax with 55mm lens.

were perfected I would add healthy, manageable hair, but with these aids, beautiful hair is a bonus rather than a necessity.

The face model can stand extreme close-ups without the need for retouching; she is generally around fifteen to twenty years old. After that, unless she is extremely fortunate, large close-ups will not be possible without some retouching. Many of the leading facial models from New York and Hollywood are over twenty, but their exceptional beauty maintains their status. Most commercial assignments prefer to avoid retouching. In color photography especially, retouching is expensive and a nuisance.

If a pretty girl has a lovely figure to go with her face, so much the better, but even with a bad figure it would be foolish to eliminate her when you could concentrate on her face.

In addition to extreme close-ups, the face model would be used for medium close-ups. She would appear on magazine covers, in beauty ads, eye-catcher brochures, and so on.

Fashion Models. Fashion models can be divided into two classifications: the very high fashion and the sports fashion. The very high-fashion model is tall (5′8″ and over), thin (110 to 120 pounds), must have a beautiful complexion and a flair for posing—and the ability to make up her face and change hair styles with a minimum of time and effort. She has style. I have worked very little with these girls on assignment. But I do like to work

Very young models from fifteen to eighteen are excellent for the teen market. Leslie Warden poses in a sylvan setting with Jim Ashley. Hasselblad with 80mm lens. A reflector filled in the shade lighting.

Andria Blahd is another fashion model whose slim, petite figure brings her many jobs as a model for youthful lingerie and feminine beauty products.

Erline Erskine has a beautiful face that does not require make-up other than a little mascara. She has a natural beauty of the classic type, which makes her an excellent subject for feminine beauty advertisements.

with them on a speculative basis where we are taking pictures creatively rather than for a specific job. A well-qualified high-fashion model is expensive to photograph, commanding fees of over a hundred dollars an hour. I have never worked with that high a fee. To me sixty dollars an hour is extravagant! I'm sure that it is worth the money, because these girls know how to pose, how to suggest ideas. They move fast and gracefully and, as a rule, love their work and look on it as a challenge.

The sports-fashion model is the girl I use the most. She is not outrageously tall, perhaps 5'6" to 5'9". She is not gaunt, but slim, with a healthy, slender, young, fresh quality rather than the exotic and often strange quality of the high-fashion girl. The face is very important, too, but with the use of make-up, wigs and falls (and because they are not called on for extreme close-ups), the various necessary facial qualities pointed out previously are not as critical. This girl is excellent for pictures on the beach, running through fields, and posed with male models.

Pin-ups.   There is a very fine line between the pin-up model and the sports-fashion girl. The pin-up girl has just a degree more roundness and is best photographed in bathing suits or brief costumes. Preferably she should be between fifteen and twenty-three—a natural beauty rather than the creation of heavy make-up. Because these girls are more buxom than the sports girl, they are used mainly in eye-catcher advertisements, calendars, and brochures. I use this girl 80 percent of the time.

Figure Models.   These are the most difficult to come by. I probably interview twenty girls before I find one I can use as a nude model. By figure model I mean a nude model. There really is no such thing as a figure model, a girl who is hired only for her figure. It is for *face* and figure always.

Probably the biggest drawback is not the attributes of the girls. Our society as a general rule frowns on girls who pose in the nude. Fortunately, in recent years there has been a trend away from this, and I am finding more girls who are happy to do figure pictures—so long as they are creative and not sexy. And the leading fashion magazines and women's journals are

Ava de la Sabliere is a fashion model who can work as a pin-up as well. She is tall and slender, but has that fresh, youthful look so necessary for glamour. Hasselblad with 80mm lens.

Paige Young has a beautiful face and figure as well. She is an excellent pin-up for calendars, commercial ads, and any assignment where the hair is featured, since hers is long, natural, and healthy.

using more and more figure studies for their beauty articles. For years Alice and I have done the majority of our nude studies as a purely creative outlet rather than as a commercial venture. There was no market for these pictures other than the photography magazines and art journals. But now, at last, the feminine figure has come into its own, and more people are appreciating the fact that a beautiful body is something to be proud of rather than to be hidden. It is something rare and unusual. If you question this, just look closely at the figures on our beaches. Most of them are too fat (many are too thin) and are out of proportion, representative of a society that prefers to overindulge and cover up the result with clothing.

Ann Cushing is an actress as well as a model so she is able to do a variety of things from head close-ups to humor to glamorous full-figure studies.

Brooke Mills is an actress as well as a dancer. She is another of my favorites because she has a natural beauty of coloring and feature, takes a serious interest in keeping herself fit and in shape, and enjoys photography. How can she miss? Her hair is a natural red, which complements her white complexion and blue eyes. Brooke is excellent either for face or figure studies.

Brooke varies the pose for this panty hose assignment. Hasselblad. One large reflector bounced flash.

Brooke models panty hose in a scene lighted with a large reflector bounced from the front and one hair light. Hasselblad with 80mm lens.

Brenda Dickson illustrates the type of beauty of face and figure necessary for bathing-suit pictures, outdoors or in. She has the lovely smile and sparkle so important to the fresh, outdoor look. Hasselblad camera with 80mm lens.

One way to keep a trim figure is to wear a brief bathing suit regularly. Girls who do this are aware of every extra pound or bulge, usually from lack of exercise, and can prevent getting out of shape by making adjustments as they go. Those who get into a bathing suit only once a year are generally so shocked and discouraged at the effort it would take to get back into trim that they give up. If a girl has a beautiful figure she is not embarrassed to pose in the nude, whereas girls who are less than perfect look on nudity with a feeling of snobbery.

In nude photography there are two classifications. The first includes subjects for calendars and men's magazines, the pin-up type. Here the girl must look into the camera; she must have a certain amount of personal appeal, a sexy quality. The other classification is the girl who is slim but not gaunt, who has a pretty face with a subtle rather than an obvious sex appeal. This is the type of model I prefer to work with for my nude studies. She is also in demand for the nude-but-not-nude advertising photography, where the client wants the girl to appear as though she is nude but covers her in strategic areas with artwork—or his product.

Now that I have categorized the various types of models, where do you find them? There are various sources. For the novice, model agencies are out. The fees are far too high for someone who is just practicing. But, if you have any talent at all, and can make up a brochure of your work, some agencies will assist you by sending you girls who need pictures. You can make an exchange deal. I still work this way with many girls who are just beginning their careers as models. Agencies, as a rule, do not have nude models, and those they do handle command double their regular fee for what they term nude modeling—even if the final result shows them "covered." They are nude but the pose or the placement of arms and legs covers their breasts and pubic areas.

There are several agencies that handle only nude models. But in most small towns there would be no such service.

Over the years I have accumulated a file of models from personal contacts or referrals by friends who know that I am in the business of glamour photography. Before I had built up a name in the field, I followed the newspapers, and when there were beauty contests or publicity photos of "Miss this or that," I would write to the girl in care of the newspaper. I would also attend various beauty pageants and many times would prefer the runners-up to the winner. It takes a variety of means to find models, but once you have made a few friends among the girls you photograph, and they are pleased with their pictures, they will pass the word along to their friends.

▶

Calendar pose showing the slender but well-rounded figure and lovely, expressive face so necessary to this market—slim but not gaunt, a pretty face with subtle sex appeal.

Calendar-type models must have excellent figures as well as pretty faces, and are usually more voluptuous than the regular pin-up or fashion girl. Looking into the camera adds sexuality.

Remember that any pictures you take cannot be used for commercial purposes unless you secure a release from the model. I use the following release form:

PETER GOWLAND
609 Hightree Road
Santa Monica, California
GL 4-7867

Date _____

In consideration of _____ , paid me by Peter Gowland, receipt of which is hereby acknowledged, I, _____
consent that you, your customers, agents and assigns, may use my name, portraits or pictures, for advertising, or commercial purposes or for the purposes of trade.

_____ L. S.

Address _____

As parents or guardian of the above named person, I consent to the above release and signature thereto and to the uses therein set forth.

_____

Address _____

Or this can be an exchange agreement. Sometimes girls will work for a percentage of sales. I did that at one time, but it is not very satisfactory, because many times pictures do not sell right away and, in the meantime, keeping track of the model is sometimes impossible.

If you get to the point where you plan to pay a girl for photographing her—with the idea that you will sell the pictures—it is a good idea to make some test shots first. Do this either when she doesn't have any photographs to show you or when you are in doubt as to the way she will photograph. This has a double advantage: you will be able to see for yourself her best angles and expressions, and, by the time you are ready for a regular sitting, there will be a rapport built up with her that will make the second session much more productive.

A test roll of model Marianne Case.

5
How To
Pose Models

The very best situation is to find yourself with a girl for whom posing is instinctive.

Posing can be taught, but I am convinced that the majority of models who have made their way to fame have been born with a natural ability to move gracefully. The girl I speak of is the one who loves working with a photographer and really needs more of a command to "wait a minute" than a suggestion of what to do.

The trouble is that a girl like this spoils the photographer who has to work with a model equally pretty but not as vibrant and enthusiastic.

The absolute worst situation is the photographer who is not familiar with posing, or does not know how to put his ideas across, combined with a girl new to modeling who stands waiting for directions.

To strike a happy medium it is important that you learn a few things about posing—enough to help your model get started.

Working indoors in a studio without props is the extreme test. I have a mirror built on wheels that I can move around behind or to the side of the camera so that the model can pose herself. Even so, there are times when this does not evoke enthusiasm. You must then make suggestions.

Begin with standing poses and work each part of the body separately. Start with the placement of the legs and feet, then the twist to the torso, the placement of the hands, and, finally, the angle of the head.

As each segment is moved into position, don't hesitate to suggest a

In a studio without props it takes a well-trained model to strike poses that are provocative and symmetrical. Candace Thayer, a dancer, is able to work easily without them. Hasselblad with 80mm lens.

This time a hammock provides a natural prop to assist Candace. Such poses seem limited, but head, arm, and leg variations are endless. Hasselblad with 80mm lens.

Sylvi Jones has such beautiful legs to go with her well-proportioned torso that a pose such as this, standing on the toes, accentuates her slimness. Sylvi faced sideways to the camera, one foot set back, and, with arms locked behind her head, swung her waist to face the camera, while rising on her toes.

With the use of a mirror the model is able to originate poses of her own, as in this case, where the lines of her torso and legs are effectively accentuated. She started on both knees and worked into the final version. Hasselblad with 80mm lens.

change if it looks stiff. I might add awkward, but many fashion layouts to-day, particularly in the high-fashion field, like an awkward look: toe shooting upward with heel on the floor, feet flat, and turned outward. But in the glamour work I specialize in I still favor poses that show a girl off to her best advantage.

While the model is standing, ask her to pivot her body so that it is not directly facing the camera. Go through a series of various arm and leg positions for that particular body angle.

When standing poses have been exhausted, go through the same routine for seated positions. Generally, you will find that even the most timid girl will by this time have relaxed to the point where she is not afraid to suggest poses of her own. One thing I do to get the greatest flexibility and variety of pictures is to shoot from all angles, moving around the model, sometimes completely encircling her.

Everything depends on your attitude toward your model. Patience is of prime importance. With patience, flattery, and a soft, controlled voice, the subject can be put at ease. She will no longer be self-conscious and will gradually get into the fun and spirit of creating a good picture. At this point the pictures will become interesting.

A system that I have used for many years is to cut pictures out of magazines and make them into a kind of portable file or portfolio that can be taken on location or used in the studio. The portfolio is something to look at to stimulate ideas. This may be thought of as copying, but after all, nothing is original. I remember a picture, taken by a well-known glamour photographer, I first saw twenty-five years ago. I recently saw the same pose in an ad with a different model, in a different location, taken by another photographer who received much acclaim for his originality. I, too, copied the pose, with another model, in a completely different atmosphere, and also received accolades for an exciting idea. In each case, however, although the same basic idea was used, the pictures did vary.

Now, rather than copying photographs from other photographers, I have built a large enough file of my own photographs so that I use my own posing guides for girls who are novices. One file has 382 ways to pose the nude. Others are pin-ups and glamour in general.*

It is easier to formulate ideas for posing and to direct when working outdoors because there are so many natural props and backgrounds to work with. The beach, of course, is my favorite location. Save the wet poses for last, because you can find more props on the sand. There are logs, fences, lifeguard towers (and lifeguards), and so on. In using props of this nature,

---

* For free information on these posing guides, write to Peter Gowland, 609 Hightree Road, Santa Monica, California 90402.

Actress Leigh Christian poses easily using the fence as a prop. The post helped make a nice composition for this portrait. Hasselblad with 150mm lens, with a reflector as a fill-in.

Ann Cushing, our versatile model, in a flattering pose. I prefer to work with girls who are not timid about posing, who need no encouragement. Hasselblad with 80mm lens.

Poses such as this are usually the result of several hours of shooting, when the model has become so relaxed that she is able to assume unique positions that are both provocative and unusual. Hasselblad with 80mm lens.

be sure that the body is placed in such a way as to have a clear area behind to avoid cutting the figure.

Another way to obtain this clear area is to shoot down, with the sand as a background. Using a top-viewing reflex camera, hold it overhead. With a 35mm single-lens reflex camera you might have to find a trashcan or log or other object to stand on in order to be high enough.

Brenda Dickson photographed in a high and low angle of the same pose. The advantage of the high angle is the absolutely clear background of sand. Hasselblad with 80mm lens.

Holding camera overhead for poses where model is lying down.

Sylvi Jones is one of my most popular models. She is every bit the outdoor girl she appears to be. I first met her when I saw her playing volleyball at the beach, something she does regularly, which helps account for that lovely figure.

Stretched-out, lying-down poses with the clear ocean as background are popular for advertising and billboard formats. The most propitious location would be just at water's edge. Not all beaches would be the same and the final placement would depend on individual locations. The beach closest to my studio has a slanting surf line so that I can pose the model on the dry sand and, by shooting directly on a level with her, the ocean becomes part of the background, with the sky taking up the rest. Both are plain areas, so they complement the figure.

POSED CANDIDS

I like to achieve an unposed look, so I generally have the model go through a series of actions like running through the surf or standing and waiting for a wave, then jumping as it hits her. But for the more subtle, unposed look, the movement can be only that of a hand, a foot, or the head. I carefully pose the figure, then at the precise moment of exposure I ask the model to kick her foot or splash her hand in the water or shake her head. It is very effective.

COMPOSITION

Now that we have explored the various methods of posing the figure, we should look into the other facet of posing, composition. We are stuck with the rectangular format, whether it is a square or an oblong, and the main thing

Many times in fashion work, a prop, as this palm frond, assists the pose as well as the final composition. Hasselblad with 80mm lens.

You can see how even the typical on-the-knees pose takes on distinction from model to model. How to get the most girl in the smallest space. Hasselblad with 80mm lens.

to remember is to fill that area with as much girl as possible. Too often, I have seen a pretty girl posed effectively, but so small in relation to the full picture that there is more scene than model. Stay close unless you want a poetic effect where the girl is merely a suggestion to an otherwise bare scene.

By composing with strong diagonal lines the camera automatically is brought closer to the model and the final effect is pleasing to the viewer. In a full length the head can be near one corner of the picture and the feet at the other.

Close cropping is something that I do regularly. You may be shooting a full length of a girl in a bathing suit, standing or leaning against something. Move in for a close-up. In doing so there are specific areas where such cropping is best. For example, try bottom framing between the neck and the bust, at the waist, just below the crotch, or just above the knees. All of

Using the white paper-roll background in the studio, the model was
photographed from a high angle in
diagonal composition.

Unusual patterns can be formed by
a nude body to create striking pictures, as in this low-angle picture,
accentuating the diagonal. Pentax
with 55mm lens.

58

Chris Boyer in an example of the full-length and the cropped close-up. Her ease and charm show off this pants suit against a plain studio background. Hasselblad with 80mm lens.

A lovely face is most important, so whenever possible I use poses that emphasize a beautiful expression, such as this reclining position. Note the effects of cropping.

Simplicity in posing and technique. Sunshine is the light source, with the white rug doubling as a reflector and as protection from the rough concrete. Model is Gina Dair. Pentax with 55mm Takumar lens and Kodachrome II film.

Using strong sun both as backlighting and as a reflector to light the shadow side of the body. Gina Dair achieves a candid quality by the white lace jacket dropped at the instant of exposure. The warm tones of her body are complemented by the blue swimming pool reflecting on the rocks behind her. The plant is an effective prop.

Studio effect featuring Diane Webber is obtained by using white seamless paper on a patio with only sunlight as the source of light. Antique chair is a simple prop. Rolleiflex.

Diane Webber employs guitar prop in this sunlight picture which exploits shadows cast by fern frond. Rolleiflex.

Pat Chapman is posed so as to fill the 35mm format. Simplicity of background derives from shooting down slightly, making use of the blue water. Sunlight backlighting with Strobonar flash fill; 4 x 5 Gowlandflex with 210mm Schneider Symmar lens.

Candid action is initiated by a garden hose while keeping the background simple. Backlighting accentuates the water spray.

Compact pose and close cropping show Pat Chapman to her best advantage. Sunlight backlighting with Strobonar flash fill; 4 x 5 Gowlandflex with 210mm Schneider Symmar lens.

This extremely high angle (a scaffold was built over the pool) provides an overall water background for this floating shot of Pat Chapman. Sunlight is the only light source. A single strand of monofilament line stretched across the pool and camouflaged by the water helped maintain the model in position. Pentax with 85mm lens.

63

Compact pose using shade
lighting aided by a gold Larson
Reflectasol. Twin-lens 4 x 5
Gowlandflex.

Working close to the subject
underwater to give the most
brilliant color. Reflection of
surface adds interest. Pat
Chapman is the model. Nikonos camera with 35mm lens
and Kodachrome II film with
a CC5R red filter.

Simple prop with distinct character adds to this picture of actress Edy Williams taken in the studio with white paper roll background and electronic flash bounced from an umbrella. Hasselblad with 80mm lens.

Making the best use of a beautiful piece of furniture by posing the model in a horizontal position. The pose also makes the model look taller than she really is. The orange quality of the lighting is due to daylight film with tungsten floodlights. Model is Patti Connelly.

Simplicity of pose and background emphasizes the beauty of the model, Merci Montello. Studio setting, using bounce strobe lights against seamless white paper. Ektachrome film, 5 x 7 Gowlandflex.

Working with window light and prop exploits the shadows to create warm body tones and lines. Hasselblad with 80mm lens and Ektachrome film.

By using a carpet hung from the wall and run under model Ava de la Sabliere, a more intense color background is obtained. It also helps the pose and provides a softer cushion than paper or the floor. A strong backlight separates Ava from the background, and a strong key light from the right adds modeling shadows to the body. Pentax with 55mm lens.

Scotsman's skirt and tam with a bikini top make an interesting costume for this picture of Brenda Dickson used in a carpet company advertisement. Carpeting was hung from wall. Pentax with 55mm lens and a single electronic flash bounced from a reflector.

A unique prop makes this picture eye-catching. The model owned this antique parasol, and the location was a quiet beach near Melbourne, Australia. Ann Hamilton is the model. Pentax with 55mm lens.

these are good cropping lines. But cropping at the feet, or the leg at mid-calf, or just at the knee makes for very bad composition.

It is possible to correct anatomical imperfections by posing. The girl with a small waist and pretty face and bust but large hips can be posed with her hips farthest from the camera, thus making them appear smaller. Also, having her hips turned at an angle so that they are not straight-on to the camera helps carry out the illusion.

If the legs are the best feature, try emphasizing them by low angles, or diagonal poses where the legs can be stretched out to their fullest, or with action that involves the legs in flattering positions.

Thin legs, posed from the back, look more shapely. The model is standing, legs either together or apart, at an almost flat-on angle to the camera, back to camera, and at the time of exposure she twists her torso, looking over her shoulder. The legs, because the calves are featured, look heavier.

The problem of heavy legs is solved by keeping them close together and turning the hips slightly to the side, one leg almost overlapping the other. If this doesn't eliminate the problem, then seated poses with legs curled up underneath the model will put emphasis on her torso and face.

ON DRESS AND UNDRESS

In glamour photography we are concerned with the girl and not the clothing; whatever she wears should complement her figure. For this reason I adhere to the simplest outfits. Brief bikinis, leotards, and lingerie are almost standard items that are the least likely to become dated and that show the figure to advantage.

Today, more than ever before, almost anything goes in the line of clothing. See-through blouses and super brief skirts are worn in public with hardly the batting of an eye. Many women are sewing their own wardrobes, and if you find a model with a minimum of talent along these lines, it is quite possible to improvise an outfit with fabric that is appropriately revealing.

In the final analysis the model will determine the outfit. If she has a perfectly wonderful figure, why cover it? If she has a pretty torso and maybe not so pretty legs, have her put on tight levis and a tight-fitting top (or nothing). If she has thin shoulders and small breasts, but an absolutely beautiful pair of legs, try having her wear a long-sleeved sweater that can be stretched to cover her torso but leaves her legs bare.

In general it is better to be underdressed than overdressed to achieve the best glamour photos.

Emphasizing the legs in a low-angled, diagonally stretched-out pose.

The model is posed leaning forward to make her hips and legs appear slimmer.

◄

Leigh Christian can pose demurely or sensually. Hasselblad with 80mm lens.

Only a girl with slim legs like Judy Swain should be posed this way, because the pose tends to make the legs look heavier.

Brooke Mills in another hosiery-ad-type pose. Hasselblad with 80mm lens.

This is as much dress as you want in glamour photography. Obviously the legs are the feature here.

Betty Samuelson is caught in her lingerie as she steps out of the dressing room. White-shuttered doors do not distract from her appearance. Hasselblad with 80mm lens and daylight only.

Brooke Mills demonstrates the advantage of being under-dressed, here and in the pictures that follow to the end of the chapter. These pictures were all taken with the same kind of lighting: two 1000-watt quartz lights bounced off two Larson Reflectasols (36-inch super silver). These two lights were connected to each other, one above the other, forming a bank of light 36 x 72 inches. The lighting came from the right side, and the model changed positions, thus giving a variety of shadow patterns. The film was Kodak 2475 recording film (1000 ASA). The exposure was 1/500 at f/8, a deliberate misuse of film to achieve the grainy effect here.

6

Basic Outdoor Lighting

The majority of quality cameras have built-in light meters that save the trouble of carrying an exposure meter and save the time and effort required for calculating exposures.

However, it is advantageous for you to have a basic idea of what various lighting conditions require as exposures. Charts are never absolutely accurate because light is never the same, but, as a general rule, so that you have some basis from which to work, I have prepared a chart for daylight exposures.

The f stops determine the size of your lens opening. The smaller the number, the larger the opening and thus the more light that stikes the negative. The shutter speed determines the length of time the film is exposed to the light. These two factors must be balanced to reach the proper exposure for your negative.

ASA	Bright Sun	Cloudy	Shade	Window Light
25	1/60 f/12.5	1/60 f/11	1/60 f/5.6	1/60 f/2.8
50	1/125 f/12.5	1/125 f/11	1/125 f/5.6	1/125 f/2.8
100	1/250 f/12.5	1/250 f/11	1/250 f/5.6	1/250 f/2.8
200	1/500 f/12.5	1/500 f/11	1/500 f/5.6	1/500 f/2.8
400	1/1000 f/12.5	1/1000 f/11	1/1000 f/5.6	1/1000 f/2.8

Early morning on an overcast day shows Leigh Christian at Malibu Beach, California. Picture was taken on 70mm film (Plus-X) with Hasselblad and 80mm lens.

Leigh at Malibu, an example of noon sun. Model tips head back, eyes closed, to avoid harsh shadows. Hasselblad with 150mm lens.

There are variations in sunlight between the darkness of a wooded area and the brightness of a beach, and there is bright shade and dark shade. But if you do not have a meter, by memorizing the above chart you will be close to the accurate exposure.

There is another consideration regarding f stop and speed. The smaller the lens opening (large numbered f stop), the greater the depth of field. That is, objects close to the camera as well as at a distance will be in sharp focus. But to use a small lens opening would require a slow shutter speed to enable enough light to reach the negative. You could use this easily where the subject is posed statically, but in the shooting of action of a model, the shutter speed must be faster so as to stop the action from blurring. In turn, the opening must be larger (smaller f stop number).

When you think of the sun as a giant spotlight, you will understand the

In a patio at high noon from a high angle.

importance of the angle of its light. The lower the sun, the flatter the light on a vertical subject. The higher the sun, the deeper the shadows around the eyes and under the nose.

Since the sun cannot be moved at will, you will have to plan your picture-taking to exploit the early morning and late afternoon sunlight. As Kodak advises: "Two hours after sunrise or two hours before sunset is the best sun for flattering angle and good color." If you shoot at sunrise or sunset there is more orange in the rays, because the sun is passing through more of the earth's atmosphere.

There are times when this orange effect definitely is desirable and, in fact, some of my favorite pictures have been made then, but remember: It is an effect, and if you want true color, avoid the extremes of very early or late sun.

Sharon Casey photographed at a public beach in California in very late afternoon sun with no reflectors. The effect is a softer shading, more flattering than with the sun at high noon. Pentax with 55mm Takumar lens.

With the sun at its noon high, the model is photographed from a high angle, reclining, with her head tipped back facing the sun. Waikiki Beach, Hawaii, with the Hasselblad.

NOON FLAT LIGHT

How can you create hard, flat light at noon? By posing your model in reclining poses with your camera held high. This will give you flat lighting on your subject because you are placing the sun behind you.

At the beach, try posing your model on the sand while you shoot from a rock or pier. You can even carry a ladder. A top-viewing reflex camera can be held over your head, which can give you a seven-foot elevation.

BACKLIGHT

With backlight, the sun becomes secondary and edge-lights the face and body, but the light you use on the camera side is your main light.

You can take advantage of many types of natural reflectors, such as light-colored buildings, sand, or even a towel. A white automobile can be a good reflector of light, if one is parked nearby. But to be sure that the reflector is the right color and that it is placed where you want it, carry your own.

REFLECTORS

A Larson Reflectasol is ideal. It can be used flat with sunlight outdoors as well as curved with tungsten light indoors. I find its silver surface works well for close-ups while its super silver throws more light when you need it for full lengths. All Reflectasols are reversible to a softer side, which reflects less light when needed.

There is nothing to stop you from making your own reflector with some plywood covered with aluminum foil, but if you want a lightweight, inexpensive, easily folded reflecting tool, try a Reflectasol.

On the beach at Southport, Australia, Peter Hill, Australian photographer, holds umbrella over the lens to protect it from the high noon sun.

The high sun back lights this portrait of Leigh Christian. Shadow area was filled in with a reflector.

Lynn Newmann, photographed with gold Larson Reflectasol, with sun backlighting, high noon. Pentax with 85mm lens.

Lynn on the beach at Southport. High noon and white sand emphasize the basic elements—the girl and the tree. Pentax with 55mm lens.

Late afternoon sun provides good backlight for silhouette of Sylvi Jones as she runs in the surf at a public beach in California. Hasselblad with 80mm lens.

Late sun, side-lighting, and no fill-in provide interesting shadows to this beach study of Sylvi.

WHY FLASH?

Everything has its advantages and disadvantages. Some models have eyes that are so sensitive they cannot help squinting when faced with a reflector. In this case I am forced to use either flashbulbs or electronic flash (strobe), even though I prefer to "see" my lighting, as with a reflector. With daylight I use blue flashbulbs. Electronic flash is already blue to match the daylight color film.

SYNCHRO-SUN

Synchro-sun is a method of balancing the flash and the sun. To help you a guide number is provided with the flashbulb or electronic flash unit for various types of films. For example, if the guide number is 66, you

Before and after pictures of Emily Oliver on lifeguard tower illustrate the use of flash (electronic strobe) to fill in shadows.

divide the distance the light is to the subject into 66 and you get the correct f stop. Six feet would be f/11.

Most electronic flash units have exposure charts incorporated in the instrument in the form of a dial that can be set at various ASA numbers, which calculates the exposure. The following chart is based on five units made by Honeywell, using Kodachrome II.

ASA 25 (KODACHROME II)

Unit	4′	6′	8′	10′	12′	20′	30′	Guide No.
100	f/6.3	f/4.5	f/3.5	f/2.8	f/2			28
220	f/8	f/5.6	f/4	f/3.5	f/2.8	f/1.9		35
332	f/9	f/6.3	f/4.5	f/4	f/3.5	f/2	f/1.4	40
770	f/18	f/12	f/9	f/8	f/6.3	f/4	f/2	80
880	f/18	f/12	f/9	f/8	f/6.3	f/4	f/2	80

The unit numbers indicate the size and the power of the unit. You can see that the larger numbered units give the most power and the greatest distance of coverage. Rather than cover the whole field of electronic equipment I have selected the one I use, Honeywell. For my work I prefer the 770 and 880 because I like all the light I can get, but for the sake of comparison I have shown the smaller units and what they can do. The 100 unit, for example, serves very well for close-up work from four to twelve feet.

Some of the units are rechargeable and some have batteries that need to be replaced when depleted. Units 100 and 220 use dry-cell pen-light batteries that can be purchased at any drugstore. The 332 and 770 are rechargeable and save the trouble of replacing the batteries. The recycling time on these four units is about ten seconds. For those who want to work faster and not wait the ten seconds between exposures, the 880 unit is the answer. Its recycle time is two seconds. This unit uses a different system: a 510-volt dry cell that will give in excess of 1,000 flashes per battery.

Once you have arrived at the correct f stop you must set your shutter according to the daylight. With an exposure meter, measure what shutter speed the daylight requires at f/11, or refer to the daylight chart provided.

With mid-afternoon sun on hilltop, model Troas Hayes is in full-length pose against a clear sky. A flash fill-in was used to avoid deep shadows. From the angle one cannot tell that this slight knoll is in the middle of a residential area. Hasselblad with 80mm lens.

Afternoon sun backlighting Merci Montello is filled in with Larson Reflectasol. Hasselblad with 250mm lens.

This synchro-sun technique is based on using a between-the-lens shutter because, as explained in the chapter on cameras and developing, a focal-plane shutter can synchronize only at slow shutter speeds.

Using flashbulbs with a between-the-lens shutter usually requires a restricted shutter setting also, in order to get the peak of the flashbulb or the most light from the bulb.

Using a comparatively slow shutter speed indoors is no problem because you don't have to contend with daylight, but for all practical purposes synchro-sun is best done with a between-the-lens shutter and electronic flash.

▶

Sylvi Jones poses in tropical setting with sun backlighting and reflector fill-in. Hasselblad with 80mm lens.

Lois Mitchell against a white wall, photographed as she came out of a swimming pool. Reflector and backlighting. Hasselblad with 80mm lens.

QUARTZ LIGHT

Using quartz light outdoors is common practice in motion-picture production. But very few still photographers seem to bother with it, probably because it isn't necessary and they can get by with flashbulbs or electronic flash for that instant exposure in making still pictures, whereas motion pictures require a continuous light source.

But the still photographer can find this continuous light to his advantage also. He can see his lighting and arrange it accordingly. He does not have to wait for his electronic flash unit to recycle (this can seem like an interminable time when one has a talented model who is rapidly changing expressions and poses), and he *knows* the light is on. With electronic flash one is not always sure if all the sync wires are working or if the flash discharges are working unless the model is asked, "Did the flash go?"

Of course with quartz light one is confined to working in an area with available electric power. The outdoors around my house—patio, garden, or front lawn—can be lighted quickly with the aid of a long extension cord.

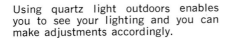

Using quartz light outdoors enables you to see your lighting and you can make adjustments accordingly.

WARM OR COLD

Daylight is blue compared to the orange of tungsten quartz, so if you are using daylight color film, your quartz light will produce a warm skin tone on the model while the background will record in its natural color. I've used this technique when taking pictures late in the evening when I want the darker blue tones of the sky and the warm skin tones of the model. When I do not want the extra warmth, I put a blue glass over the quartz light, and this corrects it to the daylight. If you are using reflected light, a blue reflector will accomplish the same thing.

SHADE LIGHTING

Working in shaded areas can produce some of the most flattering glamour studies. Shade lighting is also one of the easiest to use. You do not usually need lights, cords, and excessive equipment, leaving more time and energy to concentrate on poses, expression, and so on. To work without a tripod requires very bright shade, as on a brilliant day, perhaps next to a white building or white sand where the reflection, in contrast, can double the usual intensity of shade. Also, a comparatively fast film and lens will ensure sharper pictures if the camera is hand-held. Most experts prefer a tripod on shutter speeds under 1/100 second, but it is possible to hand-hold a camera at a shutter speed of 1/15 and 1/10. Enlargement of the film will show the difference between a very sharp picture made at fast shutter speeds and one taken on a tripod. This is especially true with very long focal-length lenses. I recommend a tripod with the combination of shade lighting and long focal-length lenses.

Since color shade-light photography depends on the color of the reflection, the photographer must be aware of what his reflective source is. I'm speaking now of natural reflectors, rather than the portable kind. For example, if the sun hits a yellow building and bounces into the shade area, the picture will have a yellow cast. If the shade happens to reflect a deep blue sky, the subject will have a blue cast. If you want these various shades, then use only those natural reflectors. If you want more natural skin tones, then you must use your own portable reflector to compensate. If you are getting overly blue tones, then use a warm-toned reflector, if overly yellow or orange, use a blue reflector.

With black and white film there is no color problem, but since most shade lighting is inclined to be on the soft side, exposure and development can be altered slightly—by underexposing and overdeveloping, the contrast of the negative can be brought up to normal. Conversely, hard sunlight negatives can be made softer with overexposure and underdevelopment.

The shade lighting in the canyon behind my studio captures Leigh Christian. The sun hitting the front of her body reflects slightly on her face. Distracting background is thrown out of focus. Pentax with 150mm lens.

Leigh is exposed for shadow area, leaving background washed out by overexposure.

7

Basic Indoor Lighting

For your most flattering glamour lighting indoors, it isn't the
number of lights you use that counts, but rather the size of the light and
how you use it. For this reason I try to use as large a light as possible. In
working with window light you must consider the imbalance between
shadow and lighted areas. Light coming from a large area makes a soft
blending between the highlights and shadows. To get the proper exposure
first, take a reading of the background (window light) and then take a
reading of the model's face. For example, if the light coming in the window
is f/16 and the face is f/4, the exposure should be in between, around f/8.

Depending on what you want to achieve, you could expose for the
background and the face would be almost completely in shadow. Allowing
slightly more exposure, the background would be washed out and the face
lighter and more detailed.

If you are using color film it should be daylight type, and whatever reflection you use should be of a blue cast. This will give balanced lighting. If
you were to use a spotlight or flood, the result would be a rather orange cast
to the face, very flattering at times, but definitely not natural. Several of the
leading glamour magazines prefer this technique because it gives a pro-
nounced glow to the skin.

Full-length pictures at window light would observe the same technique.
In posing full-length pictures you must be aware of the area behind the
model. Unless the windows are ceiling-to-floor, the light will fall off below

Model in an old garage poses by a window framed with cobwebs. Picture was taken with Pentax camera, using only the light from the window and 55mm lens.

This scene illustrates the use of window light from one side only, letting shadow area remain dark.

the window ledge, and your fill should be wide enough to fill in this shadowed area. Also, the line of body may be broken by the frame of a window or a piece of furniture. Look at the picture as a whole. Is it pleasing and uncluttered? If not, could it be improved by moving a piece of furniture, or the model, or by changing the pose slightly?

Since you can't move a window around, you can get the same effect by bouncing the light. In a pinch, you can do this by using a wall or ceiling.

Nude study is done with available light coming from floor-to-ceiling window on camera's right. Hasselblad with 80mm lens.

WALL AND CEILING BOUNCE

Bouncing floodlight or quartz light, you are able to read your exposure meter. With strobe or flash, unless you have a flash meter, you can judge the exposure by "opening up" two stops. That is, measure the distance of the strobe to the wall and then to the model and open the lens diaphragm two stops. For instance, if your combined distance is ten feet and your exposure is f/16 (normal), then open to f/8. This is based on a white wall or ceiling. Darker walls or ceiling will require a larger opening.

CONTROLLED BOUNCE LIGHT

The advantage of bouncing off a special reflector (such as the Larson Reflectasol) is that you can place the light where you want it. Since Reflectasols are usually bright silver, they reflect more light than a white wall or ceiling. Also they can be easily folded for storage and transporting. (On a

(Left) Merci Montello in bounce light from the front and (right) bounce light from the side. Hasselblad with 80mm lens.

Measuring the distance of the strobe to the wall and then to the model.

Betty Samuelson poses in sailor outfit for a commercial assignment, using available light from floor-to-ceiling window to the right of the camera. Hasselblad with 80mm lens.

Positioning a Reflectasol with quartz as the model holds a pose.

A single reflector behind the camera bounced light onto Betty Samuelson for this commercial picture with a telephone. Hasselblad with 80mm lens.

recent trip to New Zealand and Australia I carried only one Reflectasol.) They come in regular, silver, super silver, gold, and blue. The gold is very good to warm up a quartz light or for warming up the coldness of shade lighting by reflecting the sun into the area. The blue Reflectasol is used when you want to change tungsten light to daylight. This would be necessary where window light is used with daylight film. The blue reflector will make the tungsten light blue rather than orange.

ONE LIGHT

With bounce light from a large reflecting surface you can get by with only one light. Most of my glamour photographs are made with a single bounce light behind the camera. In a way, the camera is "inside" the light —light comes from all around the camera. I use a special reflector six feet across, suspended from the ceiling. It is raised and lowered with two ropes. The ropes also control the angle of the reflector so that it can be used di-

(Top) Using one light only placed behind camera. Reflector with bounce. The same pose (center), but with the head turned toward a double set of Larson Reflectasols. Same pose (bottom) with lighting coming from two sides.

95

Mary Lee Gowland poses with a single umbrella bounce light coming from the right side, with a black background. Hasselblad with 80mm lens.

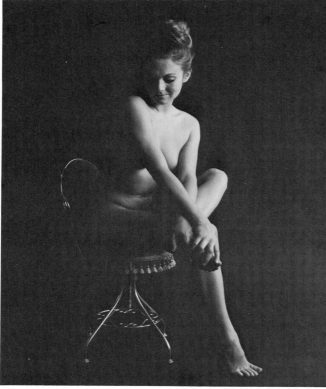

Michelle Trusello assumes a nude-but-not-nude pose on this black background study taken with one umbrella bounce coming in from the right side. Hasselblad with 80mm lens.

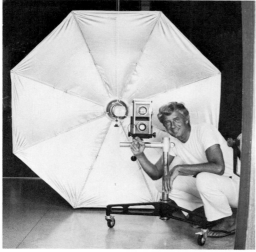

My 72-inch umbrella is hung from the ceiling. Light is 800-watt-second Ascor. A 600-watt movie light is used (shining forward) as a pilot for focusing and setting the direction of the umbrella.

The umbrella can be elevated to any level.

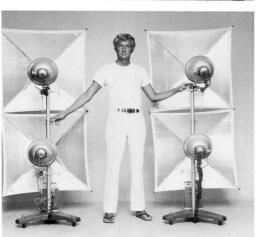

Two Larson Reflectasols are used on each rolling stand, with an 800-watt-second Ascor electronic flash unit for each reflector.

rectly on the model from the floor level or raised to the ceiling and aimed straight down on a reclining model. With a.c. cords running through the umbrella tube out the top, wires or stands can't get in the way and I can walk a complete circle around the model, shooting a variety of angles with my camera hand-held.

THE SINGLE SIDELIGHT

I also use a couple of movable lights on wheels. When I want a single light from either side, rather than move one light from side to side, I switch on one or the other. Each stand has two Larson Reflectasols mounted on it along with the 800-watt-second Ascor power pack. These lights are used six feet from the model, and since they are three feet wide and six feet high,

Example of pin-up Robin Mattson in frontlighting and sidelighting with a single reflector bounce moved from front to side.

they do a beautiful job of lighting the entire figure. When I use the six-foot reflector behind the camera, I set it at eight feet.

The "switchboard" system of lighting allows me to control the front light and two sidelights from the camera. That way I don't have to jump up from a comfortable stool every time the model turns from one side to the other. If she faces right, I fire off the light on the right. If she faces left, I fire off the light on the left. If she faces front, on goes the front light.

At times I am not sure if I want a flat front-lighted picture or a dramatic side-lighted one. Answer: I shoot both ways. I also change my lighting when using color film. Most commercial color work involving glamour models lends itself better to a flat type of lighting, rather than the dramatic shadow lighting. So if I am working with black and white and color film, I can make the changes without leaving my perch.

Sylvi Jones poses in the studio, with one light from a reflector, slightly above the camera, a strobe placed in back of the camera, and one light on her hair. Hasselblad with 80mm lens.

OTHER WAYS TO USE TWO LIGHTS

Mostly I prefer to use only one of these lights at a time. But there are times when I use two together, one sidelight on the model and the other on the background, from the opposite side. Since the second light is lighting only the background, a shield is used between the background light and the model.

Another way is to use both sidelights on the background. This is particularly good for silhouette nudes when you want the model's body in complete shadow. Shields keep the background lights from hitting the model; a semi-silhouette effect can be achieved by placement of the shields, which adds detail to the sides of the figure.

At times I use my frontlight with a sidelight on the model. This creates transparent shadows.

Profile in silhouette showing Andria
Blahd in front of a Larson Reflectasol.
Hasselblad with 150mm lens.

Using a black paper-roll background
and one umbrella light bounced from
the right of the model and one bare
strobe behind her hair gives edge lighting to the body.

Using one or two sidelights behind a screen or curtain is another way
to get the silhouette effect. By placing the model in front of the screen with
the lights coming through, her skin is dark against the white screen. This
technique can be used in lieu of a window. Behind a constructed window
seat and frame, backed with curtains, set up a bank of lights so as to create
a diffused light effect. It will give the illusion of a real window. By placing
the model on the window seat and varying the degrees of light on her body,
you will get a series of interesting silhouettes. This effect of darkened skin
against a completely white curtain is one of my favorites in nude photog-
graphy.

SIMPLE PORTRAIT LIGHTING

When dealing with a portrait, less dramatic lighting can be used. In the
whole figure both the frontlight and the sidelight create hard shadows. The
frontlight casts shadows around the edge of the figure, while the sidelight
makes one side of the body light, leaving the other dark. The area between
highlight and shadow emphasizes texture. Whereas on a full length this is

◄

Nude taken with a single umbrella coming from a low angle and to the left. Another light hits the background from the right. Hasselblad with 80mm lens.

Window light in studio, with one flood to fill in, shows humorous study of model Candace Thayer. Hasselblad with 80mm lens.

Sheryl Le Bleu was photographed with one large reflector at the right of the camera and two lights on the white background. Hasselblad with 250mm lens.

Model on floor. A single umbrella strobe was suspended from the ceiling. Hasselblad with 80mm lens.

not as noticeable, in a portrait you will have to soften shadow areas if you are going to create portraits that are flattering. This is true mainly of glamour. If you are photographing an old man you would welcome the added texture. But if this shadowy technique is used on a glamour subject it is usually necessary to retouch the area just between the shadow and the light. In the old days of Hollywood photography, many of the stars' portraits were done in this shadowy technique, with no regard for neck wrinkles or bags under the eyes. The photographer could "hit" the subject with hard spots to get as much highlight and black shadows as possible. How could he get away with it? He was using 8 x 10 film, and the star never saw the unretouched proofs, only the smooth finished product. Many times eight hours of labor went into retouching a single negative.

If you shoot large film and can retouch, it doesn't matter how hard your lighting is, but if you are working with 35mm, your lighting should be as flattering as possible. On occasion I have had 2¼ negatives retouched, but only when the head was filling the entire negative. The 6 x 7 Pentax gives a 2¼ x 2¾ negative that, when used for portraits, can be retouched.

The three-foot Reflectasol makes a simple single light for portraits. Or you can use one Reflectasol as a key light and a second as a fill-in. Or there are times when a direct 500-watt photoflood can be used as the key light and a Reflectasol as a reflector. This time the Reflectasol is used flat rather than in the parabolic shape.

Portraits are improved with a hair light. Here you can use a boom to suspend the light over the model's head. A shield will keep the hair light from shining into the camera lens. Be sure when placing the hair light not to have any of its rays hitting the model's nose.

A Reflectasol, used flat, close to model's face with floodlight.

Boom light attached to Polecat.

8

Portraits

As a beginner in photography, my first love was scenics, capturing beautiful pictures of trees and water. It wasn't long after I learned the technique of developing that my friends wanted me to take pictures of them, mostly portraits. They showed little interest in my scenics.

A photographer who can make a flattering portrait is in great demand and can command high prices. As a beginner I didn't realize how difficult it was to make a flattering portrait and didn't know how to charge for the pictures. I went about the business of making good pictures at next-to-nothing prices.

Later I learned that most people cannot accept the way they photograph. I began using tricks that I had learned from working in the movies. I had watched the camermen light the stars. I had noticed the poses, lenses, and the work of the hairdressers and wardrobe people.

At night I would set up a "portable gallery" in my living room. I couldn't afford the expensive studio spotlights, but with a gallon oil can, a magnifying glass, and a 500-watt lamp, I did have a workable spotlight. I used an old music stand to hold it up. I couldn't afford an expensive camera, so I went to Sears, Roebuck where I bought a view camera for thirty-five dollars. My lens, a 10-inch Rapid symmetrical, cost seven dollars. It had an air shutter with a long hose and rubber ball on the end, and with the slow film of 1940, all my exposures were about ⅕ second.

I think I actually made more flattering portraits then than I do now, be-

Sun backlighting the model from her left is reflected into her facial area from her right. A flattering effect is achieved by overexposing the hair (the exposure is based on the shadow part of the picture). Candid effect is achieved by the model turning her head. Hasselblad with 250mm lens threw the background out of focus, making it less distracting.

No fill-in light was used in this portrait of Cheryl Anderson. Only the sun hitting the side of her face prevents it from becoming an all-gray picture. Hasselblad with 250mm lens throws garden background out of focus. Such strong diagonal composition is unusual for a portrait.

On a bright sunny day, shade from a fence post covers part of Leigh Christian's face. Holding a strand of wheat allows the hands to be brought into the picture in a non-posed manner. In exposing for the face area the background is washed out, a desired effect with portraits. Hasselblad with 150mm lens and no reflector.

The amount of light on the subject will determine the degree of silhouette effect. Here, the light from the window, coming from behind the model, leaves her almost in silhouette. Pentax at 1/60 second at f/4.

In the tropical atmosphere of Hawaii, this early evening shot was taken against the burning torches at sunset, creating a silhouette of Susan Molina. In using the light meter I did not read directly on the torches but directed the meter slightly away from them so as not to get the brightest reading. That way the torches were a little bit overexposed and the girl's features silhouetted.

Window light coming in from the side casts light on Erline Erskine. Camera movement (uncontrollable at slow shutter speeds) caused the blurred effect, indicating the need for a tripod.

An interesting shadow effect is given to this semi-nude portrait of Andria Blahd by having the light come in only from one side. This type of lighting should be used only on models with young complexions. Otherwise any lines and blemishes are emphasized.

These two pictures were taken in the shade with no reflector. Backgrounds were thrown out of focus by use of the Hasselblad with 150mm lens. Leigh Christian wanted her various moods captured, which was attained by using the least amount of equipment—just the camera, in this case.

cause I worked hard to make ordinary people look beautiful. From the beginning I was on the right track: a soft lens, double the normal focal length, and 4 x 5 sheet film for easy retouching. In those days I only exposed about a dozen negatives, but each was carefully posed, lighted, and retouched where necessary. The subject was always pleased—or almost always.

Today I take the lazy way with a minimum of posing, hoping to make the subject look more candid. I make about a hundred 35mm exposures in rapid succession and worry little about lighting. I prefer to shoot in the shade or by a window and hope the law of averages and the beauty of the model will save me. I have only myself and the client to please. The model's opinion is secondary.

Actually, it isn't quite as bad as that. I do have better equipment today (if I choose to use it) to replace that impossible view camera that forced me to stand on my head to see my subject right-side up. I now have the Gowlandflex with a 240mm Symmar lens set. I have about three thousand dollars' worth of Ascor speedlights and all the Larson Reflectasols I need for flattering bounce light, and I am able to hire Hollywood's most beautiful models, who do not require retouching, so no wonder I get lazy and snap away with 35mm film.

Since not everyone can limit his photography to the most photogenic people and must please customers who are paying for good portraits, here are a few pointers, in addition to those in Chapter 7, that can help:

Lenses.   Use a lens that is double the normal focal length. The "normal" focal length is usually the diagonal measurement of the film format. A 35mm negative would use a 50mm as its normal lens; a 2¼ x 2¼ would be 75mm; a 2¼ x 2¾ would be 100mm; and a 4 x 5 would be 150mm. Therefore, to double these, you would use: 100mm on a 35mm camera; 150mm lens on 2¼ x 2¼, 200mm on 2½ x 2¾; and 300mm on a 4 x 5 format.

Why is it necessary to use a long lens for portraits? Why won't a normal lens do? A normal lens will work if you compose your portraits from waist up. But if you want a large head on the film, you have to move your normal lens too close to the subject. To prevent distortion your camera should not be closer than four or five feet. A long lens will give you a large head at a safe distance.

Diffusion.   A soft portrait lens is another aid to flattering portraits because skin imperfections are not recorded sharply on the film. If you do not have such a lens, diffusion will do almost the same thing. Use available diffusing glasses to put over the lens, or use black gauze.

Darkroom Diffusion.   Some photographers prefer doing their diffusion in the darkroom by using something between the enlarger and the print.

Christian Williams uses her hair as a prop (achieving a dynamic balance) in this portrait taken with floodlights against a black background. Three lights were used: two backlights and one on the subject.

Shade portrait taken with Hasselblad and 250mm lens shows
Erline Erskine against overexposed white background. Erline's hair was tossed up on top
of her head in a carefree manner, avoiding the standard, well-
groomed portrait.

With the sun hitting the model
from behind and the shade portion of the face filled in by bouncing the sun off a Reflectasol, a
most flattering type of lighting is
achieved. Close cropping was
done to place emphasis on the
eyes.

There is a basic difference in the final result, because diffusion on the camera
spreads the highlights into the shadows, giving the picture a bright effect,
while diffusion of the enlarger spreads the shadows into the highlights, giving the picture a more somber, darker effect.

Moving the Enlarger. My assistant Dale Laster has his own unique
method of darkroom diffusion. He moves the enlarger up or down during
the exposure. This prevents those unflattering lines and blemishes from
sharply recording on the paper. The picture is a soft blur.

The Large Negative. All these diffusion tricks are fine, but you can't beat using the large negative where lines and skin imperfections can actually be removed, rather than blurred. With large film you can keep the picture quite sharp and still have smooth skin. If you like, use slight diffusion on the camera also for a very flattering effect.

The problem of retouching is a good argument for the Gowlandflex, because it gives you large film (2¼ x 2¾, 4 x 5, 5 x 7) and yet it operates like a Rollei. You see your subject right-side up on the top ground glass before, during, and after the exposure. Even if the subject moves you can still keep focus and composition—impossible with a view camera.

Black backgrounds require special lighting to separate the subject from the background. Here, Judy Monterey makes a comic expression for a commercial assignment. One bare strobe behind her head separates her hair from the black background. This would be one example of an enlarged and retouched picture.

Print Retouching. Here is the last resort. If you have not covered flaws with make-up, diffusion, or retouching, you can still save the day with print retouching. This is usually done by scraping the moles and lines away with a razor blade. I hold the paper so that the area I am scraping is slightly above the table. You can do this by holding one edge of the print down with the heel of your scraping hand, while the other hand holds the print off the table. This way, the razor will not scrape away too much.

If you do remove too much you can always spot in, using the very fine spotting brush where necessary. But what about all the scratch marks from

Toni Talbot, lying in a comfortable pose, is able to react with candid actions for a casual portrait. Hair is an extremely useful prop. Larson Reflectasol with quartz light bounced to fill in the shadow area.

Toni in a changed position. Note how effectively hair, arms, and hands frame the picture.

By using an 85mm lens on the Pentax, the background in this picture of Merci Montello and her little friend Caroline Crosslin is thrown out of focus. Flowers are used as a prop to help get an animated effect by giving the models something to work with.

Another angle, with models lying on grass, but using same technique of Pentax with 85mm lens, provides variety to a series of portraits.

scraping? A good trick here is to rewet the print after scraping and redry using a ferrotype tin. This should cover most of the scratched areas.

Again, you can see the advantage of retouching a large negative instead of fooling with the print. Once done, hundreds of prints can be made, all with exactly the same high quality. Retouching prints must be done on each and every print.

Flattering Light.   If you can rely on retouching, the hard spotlight is fine. It will give a high contrast of highlights and shadows. Where the two join is the trouble area: sharp skin texture, rough spots, are emphasized (like pictures of the moon!).

With a wide, soft light, there is not much separation of highlights and shadows, and skin texture is not emphasized. Again, I recommend the bounce-light system that the Larson Reflectasols provide.

Posing.   Most portraits are taken with the subject either seated or standing upright. This means that one photographer's pictures look pretty much like another's. I try to get something different by moving the model to a lying position on the floor. I can get some interesting poses and work the hands into the composition. Also the hair can be arranged to make a more glamorous picture. An arm can support the head or the chin can rest on the hands.

The subject can be photographed from a high angle, lying on her side or on her back with her hair flowing to the side. I use a white rug in the studio and the grass, sand, or a towel outdoors.

These reclining poses not only look and are more relaxed, but the results show it.

Expression.   All the pointers thus far listed are necessary for flattering portraits, but expression is the most important. When a customer is selecting a picture of himself, his main concern is with expression. If all other aspects are perfect, the wrong expression will kill the picture for him.

Some subjects are no problem, but even top models cannot always "turn on" a good natural expression or smile. Those who try often look false. While the mouth smiles, the eyes may not. Try covering the mouth on a smiling picture sometime and see if the eyes are smiling.

With practice you can soon learn to get your subject in a relaxed frame of mind. I always ask the model personal questions to keep her mind off being photographed. (Also, I am genuinely interested.) I watch her expressions but busy myself with the camera so that she is not self-conscious. When I see a particularly good angle and expression, I start shooting. There are very few times when this does not work, at which times I generally ask about her boyfriend, and that puts a sparkle in her eye!

A single six-foot umbrella bouncing an 800-watt Ascor strobe into the face of Merci Montello with telephone is good commercial lighting. Note horizontal composition with vertical effect of hair balancing the whole. Models posed lying down are in a more relaxed attitude for portraits.

One single umbrella was bounced into the subject lying on the floor for a relaxed portrait composition. Shelly Green uses her hands to give a more natural look and to help frame this portrait. One hair light was used to bring out highlights on brunette hair.

One-light portrait of Brooke Mills. Model was lying on studio floor and one six-foot umbrella from the ceiling bounced an 800-watt Ascor strobe onto her. Note dramatic composition of hair.

This interesting approach to a "nude" portrait emphasizes the beautiful hair of Brooke Mills by using light from one side only. The lighting was window light supplemented by a floodlight coming from the same direction. Hasselblad camera.

Backlighting from the sun with garage door as a background was used for this portrait of Lorraine Zax. Face area was lighted from reflection of sun on car hood the model was leaning on. The happy expression is quite genuine. Hasselblad with 250mm lens.

Another portrait taken against a garage door. A reflector was used as a fill. This is flattering lighting, even though model Sue Beck doesn't need any help. Pentax with 85mm lens.

To try for a different angle, Leigh Christian was posed with her arms supporting her body as she leaned back from a rock on the beach. Head bent forward gives a rather intimate attitude and expression. A Honeywell strobe fills in this outdoor portrait, taken with the Hasselblad using the 150mm lens.

Pentax with 200mm lens (to throw background out of focus) captures this candid study of Candace Thayer photographed in the garden. Sun backlighting; shadow area filled in with a reflector.

9
Photographing the Nude

When it comes to using women as figure models to pose in the nude, every artist and photographer has a preference. I prefer a slim figure, unlike the buxom girl featured in the men's magazines and on calendars. The girl I use for pin-ups would qualify for a nude subject. She has a trim figure, with beautiful hands and feet. The hands and feet are featured more in nude photography than in fashion work where clothes sometimes can cover unphotogenic hands and where feet are shod.

I prefer the classic beauty for my figure photography, because even here the face plays an important part for me. I look at the face first. I like long hair, healthy and natural looking, and deplore wigs and hairpieces, although I have used these when the situation demanded it.

My experience with photographers from the Midwest or South is that they have difficulty finding girls to pose in the nude. Not that there wouldn't be girls qualified, but the rigid moral codes particularly emphatic in these areas tend to make it difficult for a girl who might want to do this type of work. That's one reason Hollywood has so many girls from all over the United States and the world. Here they can pursue careers as actresses and models, including nude models, without the harsh condemnation of society.

Lois Mitchell's trim figure and beautiful hands are exemplified in these patio shots (and the one on the following page) alongside the swimming pool behind my studio. The water drops on her body add a dimension. Note that the model looks right into the camera for a more intimate response.

Lois Mitchell. With the two preceding pictures making up this series, the progressively cropped scenes heighten a focal point. Hasselblad with 80mm lens.

I use only about two or three nude models a year. There just aren't that many girls with the necessary face and figure who are willing to pose in the nude.

There are a few Hollywood agencies (and others in film art centers on both coasts) specializing in nude models, and they have been a big help to photographers like myself. The leading fashion agencies have one or two girls who will do nude work—nude in the studio, but the pictures may show no breasts or pubic hair. These pictures are popular with the high-fashion market, and I have used this type on several fashion assignments.

Fees for these models are very high—twice their usual rate, in most cases, $132 per hour. If the client is paying the fee it is well worth it, because nothing is better than working with a well-qualified figure model. She has style, knows how to apply make-up and do her hair, and generally has a beautifully slim figure and a blemish-free complexion to match.

There are the earlier-mentioned figure models, but they qualify more for the men's magazines. These girls have sexy, well-proportioned figures and pretty, exciting faces. They look good in bikinis or lingerie.

There are no set fees for girls outside the agencies. You can discuss your project and the fee with a model before hiring her.

The classic figure—a beautiful face and body—posed on a Malibu rock ledge.
Light is overcast sun. Pentax with 85mm lens.

A black material covering a frame 6 x 6 feet was used in this picture of Candace Thayer. Lighting was daylight shade with Hasselblad 80mm lens. Curtain material was used to make the hammock suspended here between two posts in my patio. Here is the nude that is not a nude, because nothing really shows.

Same model, same prop, but semi-nude and this time shot from the opposite side, using 250mm lens on Hasselblad. Long lens throws background slightly out of focus, making model stand out.

Using white paper seamless background, daylight studio, and Hasselblad with 80mm lens for the "impersonal type" nude—the "show nothing" nude.

The advertising client may want a nude that shows nothing, as in these scenes, which were in color, with a green paper background. Though the picture was interesting in color, the green background becomes gray in black and white and is not as pleasing. Lighting is from the side with a front light used as fill. Hasselblad with 80mm lens.

The type of model you select will determine your photographic technique. If she has a pretty face, a round, well-proportioned figure, and a beautiful complexion, then perhaps you would like to try for some calendar pictures. As a rule each calendar company has its own set of standards, which usually include that the girl look into the camera with a pleasant expression. Because calendar companies prefer to work with large film, you will need to work in 4 x 5 or larger. The larger the transparency, the better your chance for a sale. For every two pictures of almost equal quality and interest, the larger one always seems to be selected. I use either 5 x 7 or 8 x 10 color transparencies for most of my calendar submissions. I might use color negatives instead when working on the beach. That is when I like to use my Gowlandflex, hand-held, with 4 x 5 and 5 x 7 color film.

While the calendar companies may demand perfection in technical quality—pictures must be sharp, well lighted, and colorful—the girl comes first. You could have the most perfectly exposed picture in the world, but if your model is not immediately striking, the picture will be rejected.

This sexy, pretty model could grace any men's magazine. Hat adds balance. Pentax with 85mm lens.

My dog Nipper becomes the prop in this calendar-type picture of Merci Montello. Single light from behind the camera. Hasselblad with 80mm lens.

The model looks into the camera, making the picture more personal. Hasselblad with 80mm lens.

Once you have your nude model, decide on the setting and lighting. I use commercial lighting techniques for the calendar nude in the studio because I want the picture very sharp and carefully lighted. I select a large-film camera such as the Gowlandflex. At times I use a view camera for 8 x 10. The Gowlandflex can use 180mm, 210mm, and 240mm lenses. My 8 x 10 camera takes a 300mm lens. All are Schneider Symmar lenses, so there is no problem with sharpness.

I prefer the umbrella system of bounce light, using my Ascor power packs with 800 watt-seconds each. I have three of these and may use a single large umbrella from the front or double lights from the side. At times both front lighting and background lighting are used. In any case, with all this power, I am able to stop down the Symmars to f/22 or even f/32, depending on the speed of the color film, and this ensures sharp transparencies.

My system is to have the distance of the umbrella or Reflectasol worked out well in advance of the sitting so that when the model arrives I don't have to waste time figuring it out, or the corresponding setting of the camera f stop. However, my front light is always eight feet from the model and when a side light is used it is always six feet from the model. This way I can change rapidly from front to side light and not have to change exposure, which is confusing every time the light is moved.

Calendar pictures tend to be flat lighted, mainly from the front, although there are exceptions. Backgrounds are also well lighted to bring all the poster color possible into the finished picture. I always use a hair light, as it not only brightens the hair but separates the model from the background.

The posed nude using single light from each side to bring out modeling in her body. Hasselblad with 80mm lens. In this artistic-nude photograph, you follow none of the calendar rules and are free to create.

Same everything, except arm is raised and only left light was used. This deepens the shadows for a more dramatic effect. Note the free use of hands and feet in this and the previous shot.

Impersonal nude of Candace Thayer using single bounce light reflector on paper background. Sometimes a picture can be for artists to draw from. Notice how the light brings the hair out of the background.

Studio props are not intended to give a feeling of reality, but rather to tell a story or give the model something to do. Not only should the model be glamorous, the prop should have some style of its own. That is why, if a chair is to be used, I try to find something interesting like a huge gold chair I borrowed from a neighbor, or a chrome wire chair from the family across the street. At times I rent an interesting couch from one of the Hollywood cinema mercantile houses. I mentally record every piece of interesting furniture at neighbors' and friends' homes for use at a later date. A Mexican chest, an interesting mirror, a French brass scale will all be used. An interesting prop will contribute to a model's enthusiasm and creativity.

My studio technique is changed only slightly for a room setting. Depending on the size of the room, I might use small reflectors, but I usually use electronic flash bounced off a Reflectasol. Also my exposure is based on measured distance and the corresponding f stop for that distance. Electronic flash is balanced for daylight, so daylight color transparency film is used, which in the magazine and calendar business is preferred to a negative.

For a change, I sometimes use tungsten light, which requires tungsten color film, or quartz lighting. Bounce light does not offer the possibility of "seeing" your lighting before you take the picture, while tungsten lighting does. Also with small spots you can get tricky and light various sections of

A part-of-the-body technique. Her fingers are part of the "prop." Window light was used with 80mm Hasselblad.

Window light in my studio, a white background, and a single prop were used for this artistic-type nude. Hasselblad with 80mm lens.

the body such as the face, bust, and legs. This way each section is lighted for maximum flattery. For example, if the legs are heavy, they can be shadowed.

Calendar nudes in outdoor settings should have a commercial-type lighting, with the girl looking into the camera. The background should be sky, because frequently it provides the greatest expanse of concentrated tone. Pose the figure so that the entire body is in the picture. In most cases the model will be seated, because standing poses of necessity require the camera to be at a greater distance from the subject, thus reducing the figure.

When shooting outdoors I work out my lighting in advance, using either a reflector or electronic flash. I have two distances worked out for the

▶

This figure is ideal for an artistic pin-up or calendar-type nude. The entire body is used, with a hat prop and water background. Overcast day. Pentax with 85mm lens.

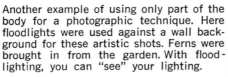

Another example of using only part of the body for a photographic technique. Here floodlights were used against a wall background for these artistic shots. Ferns were brought in from the garden. With flood-lighting, you can "see" your lighting.

flash, depending on whether the sun is front- or back-lighting the subject. If front-lighting, I use the flash at ten feet. If the sun is back-lighting I use the flash at seven feet. The exposure is usually 1/60 second at f/18, Daylight Ektachrome, ASA 50. The electronic flash is Honeywell 200 watt-second light output.

Opposed to the commercial calendar nude is the extremely artistic nude —slim and well proportioned. There are no rules to follow, such as the model looking into the camera at all times, or the necessity for particular backgrounds and colors. You can use all or part of the body to create interesting patterns or contours. In doing an article with an astrological theme, I photographed various models in sections, indicating a particular portion of the body ruled by a particular planet. It was an unusual presentation. In the artistic-nude field, you are free to create.

At such times, I use lighting sparingly. I prefer the shadowed figure, and the contours of the body should be embellished by only one or two lights. Many times I find the harsh sunlight outdoors preferable. By placing the model at different angles to the sun, the shadows will fall into different places, or with the sun in back of her she can approach the silhouette, de-

Candace Thayer posed on carpeting laid on patio surface to make use of sunlight, which was weak. This noontime shot was taken from a ladder both to obtain the overall rug texture for the background and to minimize shadows.

Kathy Davitt in the grass on a Queensland, Australia, beach. Close cropping and horizontal pose emphasize her lovely back and beautiful face. Pentax with 55mm lens.

Unique use of water and sky in this low-angle shot provides a striking foreground and background.

A soft-focus effect using a Roden-stock Imagon lens on a Gowlandflex camera. Strong sunlight backlighting gives a halo effect to lovely Edy Williams and helps reveal her figure through the see-through top.

Dancer Lisa Hamilton photographed at sunset. By placing model in a direct line with the sun, her body stands out in silhouette against a blazing sky.

Shooting almost straight down from a mounted scaffold provides an un-cluttered background, with the red suit making a striking contrast. Shadows are cast by a late afternoon sun. Model Pat Chapman was held in place by a monofilament line.

Close cropping of bikini-clad Sylvi Jones makes full use of a 4 x 5 transparency. Illumination by sunlight with a flash fill.

A simple prop, a piece of seaweed, aids Edy Williams in showing her beautiful figure. Full-length poses such as this feature the legs and waistline. Late day shooting gives an orange cast to the picture.

Kathy Davitt at a Queensland, Australia, beach. With the tide out, reflecting the model on the wet surface becomes possible. Note how the low angle brings in the sky in an almost continuous tone. Pentax with 85mm lens.

These plastic stools were used to add color, but the end result is too staged. The lovely model Reagan Wilson needs very little assistance. Pentax with 85mm lens.

Compact cropping of this horizontal pose emphasizes the beautiful torso of Sylvi Jones. Low angle gives clear ocean and sky background. Honeywell Strobonar flash, Gowlandflex.

Action is supplied by the movement of the water. Model Diane Varga was posed first and waited for the wave to break. Late afternoon sun provides flat lighting. Pentax using telephoto 200mm lens.

136

Jackie Hewitt reacts to the swirling water around her legs. Honeywell Strobonar flash fill-in, 4 x 5 Gowlandflex.

Calendar-type pose. Low angle captures the blue-sky background, orange bikini is for complementary color, and model leans forward to emphasize the bust and to minimize the stomach and hipline. Flash fill-in, 4 x 5 Gowlandflex.

For stimulating backgrounds for figure poses, this sandstone formation creates a perfect spot for the model. Extremely late afternoon sun provides a flattering light; Gowlandflex.

138

Australian model makes an impersonal nude with a horse as a prop. Overcast daylight with Pentax and 85mm lens.

In this shadowed figure the contours of the body are highlighted by a single light source, the sun. Black paper background, single bounce Reflectasol from camera right, and flower for a prop were used for this impersonal, artistic semi-nude. Hasselblad with 80mm lens.

Candace Thayer uses a top hat as a prop at Malibu Beach to form this impersonal nude at sunset. Sun is behind her. Hasselblad with 250mm lens.

White plastic over wood frame makes a background for soft light on these pictures of Erline Erskine. Hasselblad with 250mm lens. Note how entire figure is caught close up by use of the seated pose.

pending on how low the sun is on the horizon. Soft lighting is flattering to the semi-nude figure. I have built a framework of white wood over which is stretched opaque plastic. Sometimes I use this indoors and at times carry it to the garden for use as background to create a soft, white, feminine setting. At other times I use bedroom settings, particularly if there are window areas with soft, feminine curtains or fluffy rugs. The light from the window casts shadows on the body, much as a side light from the studio set-up.

The greatest difficulty in photographing the nude outdoors is finding a location. You may have to drive miles to find a private area. At a beach you might have to walk a mile or so to get away from people, and that means hauling equipment as well. But I prefer even this to indoor pictures, including garden settings. At the seashore, in a field of flowers, or a shaded glen, the combination of nature's beauties with a beautiful figure is hard to beat.

10
Working with Water

Something magical occurs in combining a model and water, and there are many sources of water—rain, ocean, pool, lake, even hose water.

My favorite location is the beach, with its ever-changing tides and waves. Living close to the ocean, it's little wonder that I take advantage of its many moods. When the tide is out, an expanse of wet sand beautifully reflects whatever traverses it, or stays to pose. Waves breaking close to shore, wild and unruly, set a scene.

I like to do my shooting either in the morning hours or late afternoon when the sun is lower on the horizon. I begin with dry poses and finish up with a completely wet model.

Such a working schedule is necessary, and it is surprising what a difference a plan makes. For example, wet hair would cancel dry-sand poses because it won't look as good; also, for close-ups, the hair has been ruined. Once you become aware of these limitations, you can overcome them and be assured of a variety of pictures.

I start with the model standing in the shallow surf and have her go through a series of small actions, like running in the low tide, either across or toward the camera. Then she goes deeper into the surf, perhaps waist deep, and a few waves splash her, causing her to jump, perhaps, to escape, or I'll catch one flat-on of a huge splash around her. Finally, I'll have her lie down in the shallow water, completely immersed, while the waves roll over her.

Sharon Casey poses on wet sand that catches her reflection. Note diffused background. Pentax with 55mm lens.

Another example of using the wet sand as a reflecting surface. Pentax with 55mm lens.

Nude photographed from a high angle captures the sparkle of the sun reflected in the water. Sun behind the model puts her in a near silhouette. This picture was taken in Australia with a Pentax camera and 55mm lens.

With the camera at a high angle and Leigh Christian walking in the surf, one gets the feeling of movement, while the water becomes a complementary background for the model. Overcast day required a flash fill-in. Hasselblad with 80mm lens.

Actress-model-writer Jeanne Rainier reacts with pleasure to a splash of cool water. Hasselblad with 80mm lens caught the water pattern by using a strobe (Honeywell Strobonar). Note how the diffused background accentuates the subject.

Erline Erskine was first posed leaning on a rock when the water had receded, and the shutter was pressed at the moment a new wave broke. Her startled expression is a natural reaction to the sudden dousing. Hasselblad camera with 80mm lens.

Cherie Close frolics in the ocean water, alone and with a friend. Camera was the Nikonos 35mm, which can be used as an underwater and a surface camera.

For all this wet work I try to use either a telephoto lens or a waterproof camera. Or I put a filter over the lens to protect it from the water, which can easily mar it. I work in the surf with my Hasselblad, but I've learned to judge the waves so well that I can snap the shutter and immediately raise the camera above my head without getting it wet. But I wouldn't advise this for a beginner. I sometimes use the Nikonos, an underwater camera (35-mm) that can be used just as easily above as below water. But I restrict its use to above water, when working extremely close, as in the shallows when the model is lying full length and I want my camera low.

Using water as action for a picture, Sylvi Jones posed on the sand and raised herself up when the wave rolled in. Hasselblad with 80mm lens.

Another favorite water location is the nearby stream that runs directly in front of my property, which is on the bank. The stream is only ankle deep and very clear, and the accompanying watercress and other greenery make picture-taking a pleasure. There is one section where the water cascades in a fall of about four feet, where I like to pose the model—in front, under, and beside. Here, too, the model not only must look pretty, she cannot be afraid or uncomfortable in water.

The difficulty of working in this location is the rush of falling water, which makes communication with the model a strain. After a while this can become exasperating, with Alice acting as a runner between photographer and subject, passing along my instructions. When the sun hits the stream around noon it adds sparkle and much excitement. I generally work with strobe or a reflector because the sun is almost directly overhead.

With a pool setting, constant awareness of the background is necessary. In most cases, the photographer is limited to shooting down, with the clear pool as a background. Otherwise there is the possibility of clutter—part of a house, shrubbery, and the like. I've always hoped to have a pool located

A technique used in the surf is to shoot into the sun and have the subject leap out of the water as the wave hits. The star effect is from the water on the lens of the Instamatic underwater camera used to take the picture.

Model and horse are posed so that the water becomes the background. Because the day was overcast, the surface of the water was light and shimmery. Pentax camera with 55mm lens.

Another method of using the water as a background is to have the model floating or swimming and shoot from a high angle. Hasselblad with 80mm lens.

Water caught in motion by a fast shutter —1/500 second—makes a lacy pattern around the model. It would have been better to have a clear background. Hasselblad with 80mm lens.

When using a swimming pool, the difficulty is getting a clear background for the model. Here, Lois Mitchell's head is too closely connected with the cluttered background. Hasselblad camera with 80mm lens.

A good background for the figure and face was obtained by shooting with the camera at a higher angle so that the water alone is the background. Hasselblad with 80mm lens.

148

The water droplets on Lois's body and the wet hair add depth and interest.

on a hill so that the edge blends in with the blue sky. But our concern is the use of pool water, and so the pictures will be taken from a high angle, or underwater, with the model submerged. Or the model can jump up from the shallow end, arms outstretched, splashing water and creating a partially diffused background. This is when I'd like that pool with the edge that goes into infinity. With the head wet and thrown back we have a direct copy from a famous picture, but I still love to try it with different models because it varies every time.

In going underwater, I try not to unduly disturb the water's surface which, when photographed from the bottom of the pool, acts as a mirror for the model. Many weird and different patterns can be made this way. I seldom, if ever, use an underwater scuba tank. I like to submerge just a second before the model does, get myself positioned on the bottom of the pool, and then have her slowly sink to a predetermined spot. I can often take three exposures before resurfacing for air. How do we sink so easily and remain on the bottom? The secret is in hyperventilating before diving. You take a series of quick breaths, then exhale as much as you can. The exhaling permits you to sink easily because the lungs have been emptied, but only partially, because there is still enough air left to permit you to stay for up to thirty seconds, even a minute.

The best underwater pictures are taken at close range. This is true of the ocean or the pool. Rarely have I found water clear enough to produce sparkling full-length pictures. There is usually so much density to penetrate that full-length exposures made at greater than five feet are blurred.

To help add contrast to black and white film underwater, I use an orange filter. Even so, the filter does not correct at distances over five feet. With color film I apply a CC5 to a CC20 filter, depending on how much correction is needed. Check the film package for the numbered filter. The exposures are determined by my Sekonic underwater exposure meter, but a general rule of thumb is that underwater exposures are two stops beyond above-water exposures.

In working with an underwater model, long hair makes for more interesting pictures. It can also get in the way. Shooting the model diving toward the bottom will keep her hair in a flowing pattern, away from her face, but once she stops, the hair is unpredictable and it will finally cover her face. If you are prepared, you can catch the hair swirling off at different angles—rather than covering the face or back.

Most of the girls I have used underwater have the ability to keep their eyes open and even their mouths slightly open when under, and if it were not for the shadows cast by the sun—with the movement of the water—it would seem they were above water.

Speaking of shadows, I like to use the pool when the sun is hitting it at an angle rather than directly overhead, because this provides different back-

Working with Cherie Close in the pool with the Nikonos camera, which uses an accessory view-finder underwater. Because of the mask the camera-man couldn't bring a regular viewfinder close enough to his face.

With the cameraman waiting at the bottom of the pool, Cherie has jumped in feet first, creating bubbles all around her body as she sinks, making an interesting effect.

Taking readings of the face with the Sekonic underwater meter. Note the Rollei Marin housing with the Rolleiflex camera.

grounds. There are the dark shadows of the shade or the shadows created by the movement of the water. I avoid underwater pictures on overcast days because the water has no definition, and if it were not for the floating hair one might not even be able to detect that the picture was taken underwater.

Underwater pictures in the ocean or lake require a light bottom and depths of ten feet or less. Any lower and the light problem increases; it may even require flash. Also, at these depths, you and your model will need underwater breathing equipment, which obviously will ruin your model's appearance.

Finding clear water requires looking. The Bahamas and parts of Hawaii, Florida, and Southern California suffice very well for underwater glamour studies.

If there is no water available, how about artificial rain? I've used it for photographs to illustrate a book of poetry. I built a rack to hold five one-gallon cans that had holes punched in their bottoms. I filled the cans with warm water so that the models wouldn't get too cold. A garden hose or cold water would do just as well if the weather is warm enough. However, I made the mistake of punching the holes in too regular a pattern, and the rain looked far too uniform. It worked well enough, but it could be improved with irregularly sized and spaced holes.

When the sun is directly overhead, interesting light patterns are cast underwater on the walls and bottom.

When the sun hits the pool at an angle, the shade side becomes a clear blue without the sun patterns. In both scenes the side is blue and the bottom still retains the reflections. Cherie (left) sinks to the bottom, blowing bubbles, and (right) the force of her falling body creates the bubbles.

153

Couple embracing under a shower of water printed in reverse for interesting effect. The rainmaker was built especially for the picture. Five one-gallon cans, with holes punched in the bottoms, and then filled with water, were supported above models' heads.

Unfortunately most of my bathing-beauty assignments come in winter when the water is sometimes 55 degrees and lower. Just the slightest touch of her toe and the model breaks out in goose bumps. As much as I try to avoid it during the colder months, when I have a rush job and cannot postpone it, I work a model in the ocean but take every precaution to see that the job goes smoothly.

First I select a girl with a fairly rugged constitution and who does not mind the cold; someone who likes to ski as well as swim. Though uncomfortable, she may even enjoy the challenge, looking upon her assignment as an adventure and not a job. If the sun is out, half the battle is won. If there is a minimum of wind, that's even better. But if it's overcast and windy, then we're lucky if we end up with good, lively pictures. Even so, we've done it, and that's where the second requirement comes in. With a series of pictures in mind, there is very little pausing to think, and so we talk it over beforehand. We carry warm clothing and big towels, and at the last minute the model goes through her poses. I do all the dry pictures first, in between letting her keep warm with a big fur coat that Alice keeps for the purpose. The wet pictures are done in a matter of minutes, and once the model is fully wet usually she can stand the cold longer than when she was just wading. Immediately after finishing I wrap her in a towel, give her hot coffee from a thermos, and return to the studio.

11
Action!

The most exciting phase of glamour photography is the action picture. Strangely enough, it is one of the easiest to take.

I was about to add, "provided you have the right model." But that isn't exactly true, because I have taken some of my best action pictures with girls who were neither glamour nor action models. It just happened they were able to carry out a piece of action that resulted in a picture.

But if you want to avoid extra work, be sure to get the best action model you can. This way almost every exposure will be a winner rather than one in a hundred.

Look for dancers or the athletic types. Dancers are trained to be graceful, and physically active girls have the power and control to carry out an action idea. Both can work from sunrise to sunset without tiring. Not only are they uncomplaining, but most dancers and active models are eager to take pictures, partly just for the love of doing it and partly because they can use a variety of pictures in their portfolios.

Outdoor Locations.   To give my action model the space she needs, plus a background without distractions, I usually try to find a beach where the sand is flat and hard and where there are not too many people to get in the way or inhibit her.

At times I use a park at an incline, so that I can place my camera low enough to use the sky as a background. But any place you find that meets the requirements will do.

Indoor Locations.   Unless you have studio space, action indoors can be a problem. In my studio I built a seamless plaster background, sixteen feet wide and twelve feet high, with a two-foot-radius curve at the ceiling and the floor. The white plaster connects with the white terrazzo floor. The ceiling curve allows me to shoot from low and high angles without getting a line at the top or bottom of the picture. A leap makes the girl look as though she is in space, with no lines interfering with her body. At one time I used paper rolls, but they slipped when the model moved or jumped, which could be dangerous.

Some photographers use a curved sheet of linoleum instead of the plaster, and have good results. Even plywood could give the same effect; just work it into a curve and paint it.

Indoor Action Lighting.   For good all-round action lighting, use four lights on the background—two on each side—with one key light on the model.

These five lights can be electronic flash (strobe), quartz, or floods. Electronic flash will give you more of an action-stopping light, but you can achieve the same effect with floods or quartz if you use a fast film.

The five-light system will give you the poster effect, because the background is lighted separately from the model, making her stand out from it.

Camera Angles.   I usually shoot indoor and outdoor action from a low angle, featuring the model's legs for dancing shots; it makes her appear higher on leaps and jumps. Outdoors, the low camera puts the model more into the sky.

The reflex cameras are best here, such as Hasselblad and Rollei and 35mm cameras with top viewing. The rear-viewing SLRs can be fitted with a top-viewing finder, so that it will not be necessary to lie on your back or stomach to get low angles.

Shutter Speeds.   Action pictures are usually made with the faster shutter speeds, 1/400, 1/500, or 1/1000 second, to freeze action.

The ability of a shutter to stop action depends also on the direction of the movement—whether it is moving toward or away from the camera, or across. Toward and away can be stopped with a slower shutter, 1/125 to 1/250, whereas across-action requires the faster shutter speeds of 1/400, 1/500, and so on.

There is also "peak" action, which can be stopped with the slower speeds. An example of peak action is a jump. The subject leaps into the air, the shutter clicks, and the model drops, having been captured in that split second when the action stopped because her movement changed direction.

Shooting outdoors on a sunny day. Troas Hayes was asked to run toward the camera. Low angle provides a clear-sky background.

Working with daylight only, in the studio, the feeling of action is simulated by this pre-planned pose of the model rolling over a hassock.

Fashion model Andria Blahd gives a slight swing to these filmy clothes, creating interest-ing action pictures of these couturier designs. Lighting was via Reflectasols that bounced strobes against a white paper roll. Exposure ASA 125, 1/200 second, at f/22.

A single umbrella with strobe placed over the camera stops the action of the leather fringe on model Ann Cushing. Ex-posure ASA 125, 1/200 second, at f/22. Hasselblad.

Examples of slow and fast shutter speeds. Taken with a Pentax camera at Malibu Beach, California. Model moves across the camera. The difference is between a 1/500 second and 1/15.

Susan Beck leaps against background of waves and is caught at the peak of her action at 1/250 second with the Pentax camera.

Brenda Dickson tries to stand still while a wave splashes against her. Action is provided by the movement of the water rather than the model, who remains in perfect focus. Exposure ASA 40, 1/250 second, at f/8.

This could be stopped with a shutter speed of 1/60 or 1/125. It takes a little practice to train yourself to know when to make that click. If you have the subject make a few trial leaps you can learn to anticipate the exact moment.

There are times when a blurred effect is desired. There are two different ways to do this. One is to pan the camera with the movement so that the subject is sharper than the blurred background. The other way is to keep the camera still so that the background is sharp and the moving subject is blurred. The slower the shutter the more blur. Try 1/15, 1/30, and 1/60. This technique used with black and white film is interesting; color film is even more fascinating because the colors blend together, like dyes in water.

You should be selective about the action pictures you take. For instance, it has never worked for me to photograph a dancer's routine from beginning to end. There are only a few highlights that deserve recording on film. You can find these by having the dancer go through the routine and stop her when you see what you feel would make a good picture. It may take several exposures on a special pose or action to get what you want. And there is always the unexpected—you never really know what the camera caught until the film is developed.

While the model was running toward the camera, birds gathered, and she startled them into flight, making a nice foreground action. Exposure ASA 40, 1/125 second, at f/11.

So far I have been concentrating on dramatic situations. There are the many other opportunities to add action to your pictures without the use of professional dancers.

Work on the beach with an athletic model. I generally pose the first few pictures very carefully while the girl's make-up is still fresh and her hair looks fairly neat. Then I call for subdued action, where the model may be seated in the surf and will move an arm or a leg, or raise herself up to miss the splash of the water. She could roll in the low tide, splash the water with her hands, and toss her wet head back and forth. These are all subdued actions that give a picture a spark of life.

Later in the sitting, as a finale, I'll ask her to run in the surf, alone or with a male partner. A male model can often lift the girl, carry her on his shoulders, or swing her around.

There is the natural action associated with sports, such as volleyball, tennis, and skiing (water and snow). The same rules apply. Study the action first to make sure of the best possible angle and camera location. In volleyball, the beach courts are the best because it is possible to shoot in a direction that will put the subjects against a clear sky background. In water-skiing

A kick of the foot. . . .

you will need a boat. Some of the best water-skiing pictures I've seen were taken from a special platform built on a speedboat. I did some water-skiing pictures of an airline stewardess in Hawaii, but I had her going up a ramp and caught her as she came off. I was positioned in a boat off to the side and used a telephoto lens; I didn't want to interfere with the action of the pilot boat.

Alice and I are always testing our imaginations to see what unusual situation we can work with. We know that nothing is new, but with a different model and a varied setting, a familiar action looks different. A successful series we did was of a girl rolling down a grassy bank. She was wearing a short, flimsy nightgown, with panties to match, and because she had dance training she was able to hold her arms and legs in graceful poses as she rolled. We once had a girl riding a bicycle in the surf, and one girl kept jumping on a trampoline, the kind used in stunt work.

With a little practice you can come up with even better ideas for action.

. . . and a splash with the hands make effective action shots.

In the countryside of Australia this girl and her horse are completely backed up by the small stream. Shot with a Pentax at 1/500 second, the girl went through the action several times to get the largest volume of water caught in the air.

This young couple running over a bridge was a rehearsed action, taken at 1/125 second, causing the boy's head to blur as well as the girl's hands and feet. Pentax camera.

Jackie Hewitt runs toward the camera, feet splashing water to create a further feeling of action. Note the clear-sky background. Shutter speed was 1/500 with Pentax camera.

Daylight from studio window coming over a black background hits the hair and side of Brooke Mills. A reflector fills in shadow side. Pentax caught the bursting of a bubble on her little finger at 1/125 second.

To stop the action of the water in these pictures took an exposure of 1/500 second. The model went through this action of flipping her head out of the water several times. Each exposure caught her hair at a different stage of the action.

Index